AF813112

# Microsoft Project 2013 Advanced

Michelle N. Halsey

ISBN-10: 1-64004-138-9

ISBN-13: 978-1-64004-138-7



Silver City Publications & Training, L.L.C.
P.O. Box 1914
Nampa, ID 83653
https://www.silvercitypublications.com/shop/

Contents

# Chapter 1 – Getting Started

Welcome to the Microsoft Project 2013 Advanced tutorial. Project is a sophisticated project management software that can help project managers with planning, assigning resources, tracking progress, managing budgets, and analyzing workloads for projects.

Microsoft Project allows you to monitor, update, and create many facets of project development. It allows managers to track budgets, completed and pending tasks, look at overall progress, and see the big picture of the project as it is advancing.

Research has consistently demonstrated that when clear goals are associated with learning, it occurs more easily and rapidly.

By the end of this tutorial, you should be able to:

- Split the view
- Sort, group, and filter tasks
- Use zoom
- Overlap, delay, or split tasks
- Set task deadlines and constraints
- Understand task types
- Assign a task calendar
- Understand task indicators
- Assign a resource calendar
- Customize a resource calendar
- Apply predefined resource contours
- Specify resource availability
- Group resources
- Enter resource rates and overtime rates
- Specify pay rates for different dates
- Apply a different pay rate to an assignment
- Use material resource consumption rates
- Entering task fixed costs
- Schedule resource overtime
- Identify and balance resource over-allocation

- Save a baseline plan
- Update project, actual task values, actual work and actual costs
- View project statistics and costs
- Check duration variance, work variance, and cost variance
- Identify slipped tasks
- Save an interim plan
- Customize a basic or visual report
- Create a custom report
- Sort a report
- Inserting a subproject
- Consolidate multiple projects
- View multiple project critical paths
- View consolidated project statistics
- Create a resource pool

# Chapter 2 – Viewing the Project

In this chapter, you will learn some advanced ways to view a project. You will learn how to split views to look at different information at the same time or use the Task Form for entering task details. You will learn how to sort, group, and filter information, including using AutoFilters. Finally, you will review how to use Zoom.

## Using Split Views

Use the following procedure to setup split views.

Step 1: Select the **View** tab from the Ribbon.

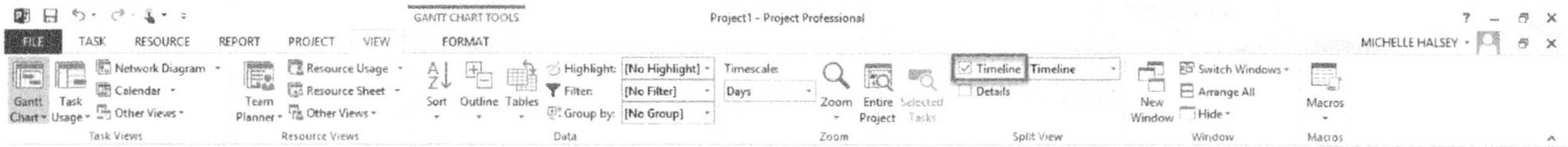


Step 2: You can show the Timeline or another view in the split window. To show the Timeline, check the **Timeline** box. The Timeline portion of the screen is displayed at the top. You can change the bottom view using the other View tools just as you would if the Timeline is not displayed.

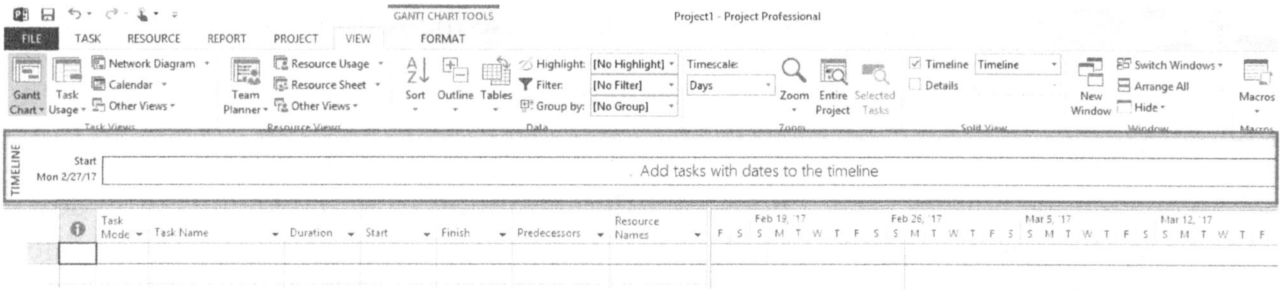


Step 3: To show a detail view in the split window, check the **Details** box on the **View** tab of the Ribbon. Select the desired view from the drop down list.

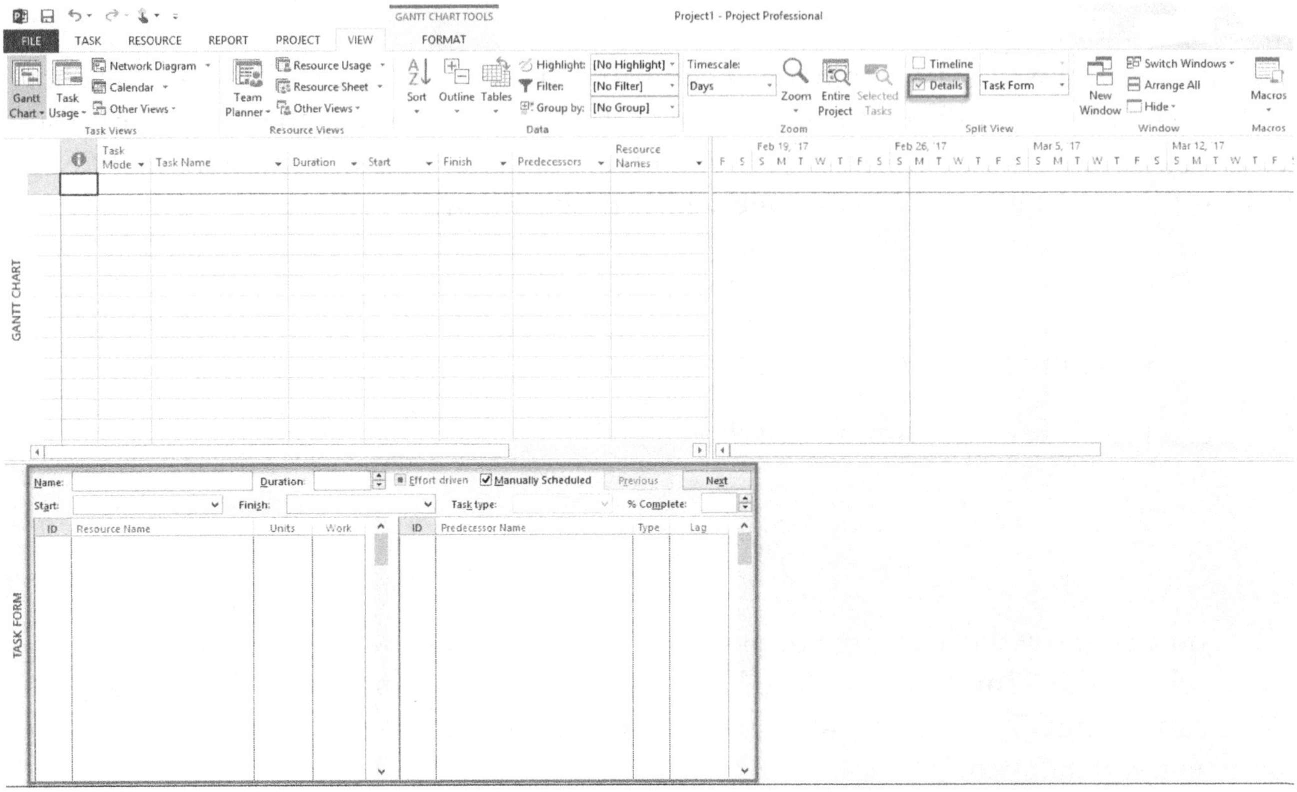


To change the view displayed in one of the split areas, use the following procedure.

Step 1: You can change the top view by selecting the desired view from the **View** tab on the Ribbon.

Step 2: To change the bottom view, choose a different option from the Details drop down list in the Split View area of the View tab on the Ribbon. Or you can right-click the title bar on the left and select the desired view from the context menu.

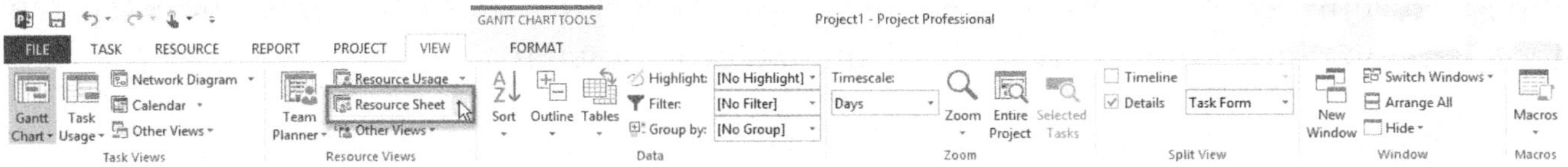


To remove a split, use the following procedure.

Step 1: Uncheck the box in the Split View area on the View tab of the Ribbon to remove the split.

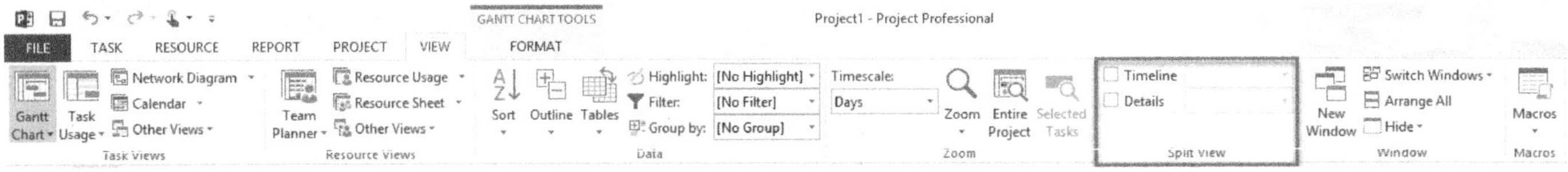


Project removes the bottom view and expands the top view to fill the window.

## Sorting Information

Use the following procedure to sort tracks.

Step 1: Highlight the tasks that you want to sort by selecting the row number. You can click and drag tasks that are next to each other or you can press the Ctrl key while you click the different rows.

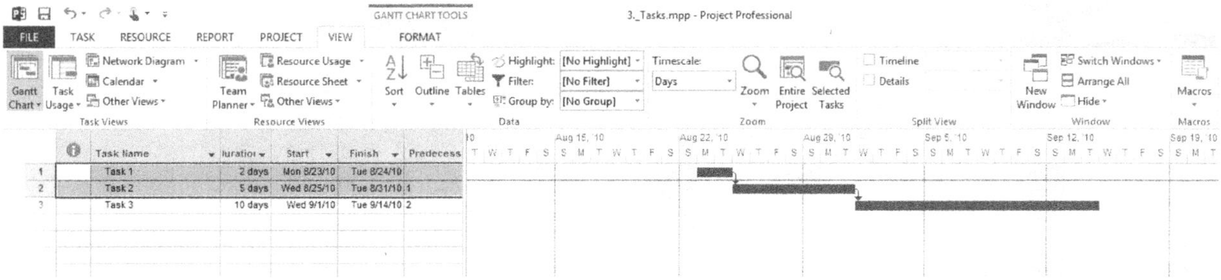


Step 2: Select the **View** tab from the Ribbon.

Step 3: Select **Sort**.

Step 4: Select one of the sorting options.

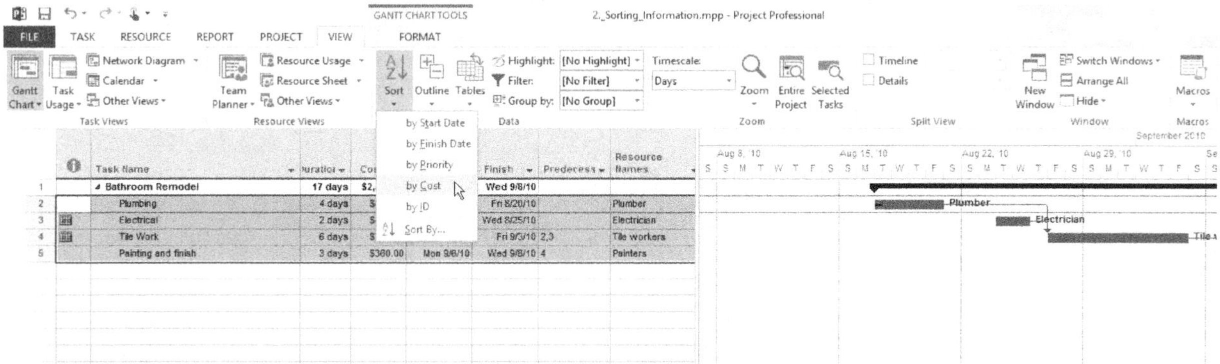


Project rearranges the tasks according to the sort option you selected.

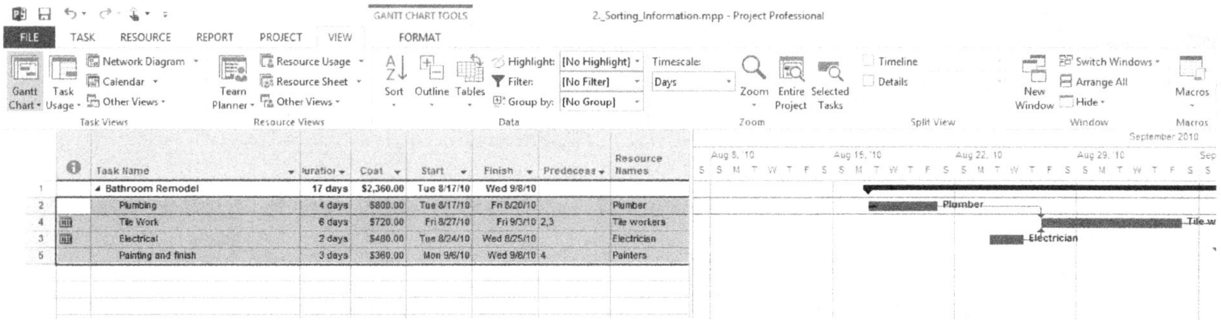


The *Sort* dialog box can be accessed by using the following steps.

Step 1: Select **Sort** from the **Project** menu. Select **Sort by**.

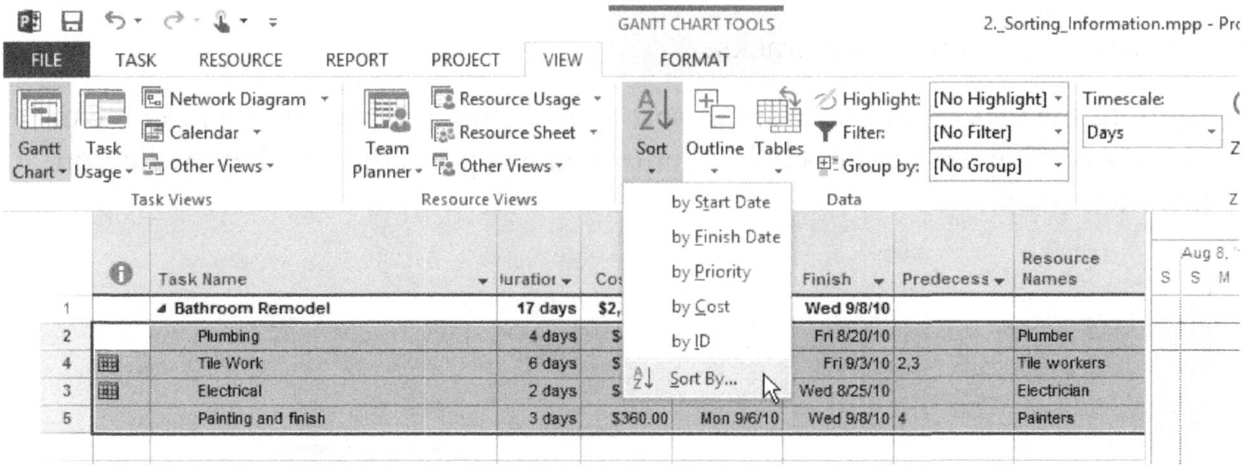


Project opens the *Sort* dialog box.

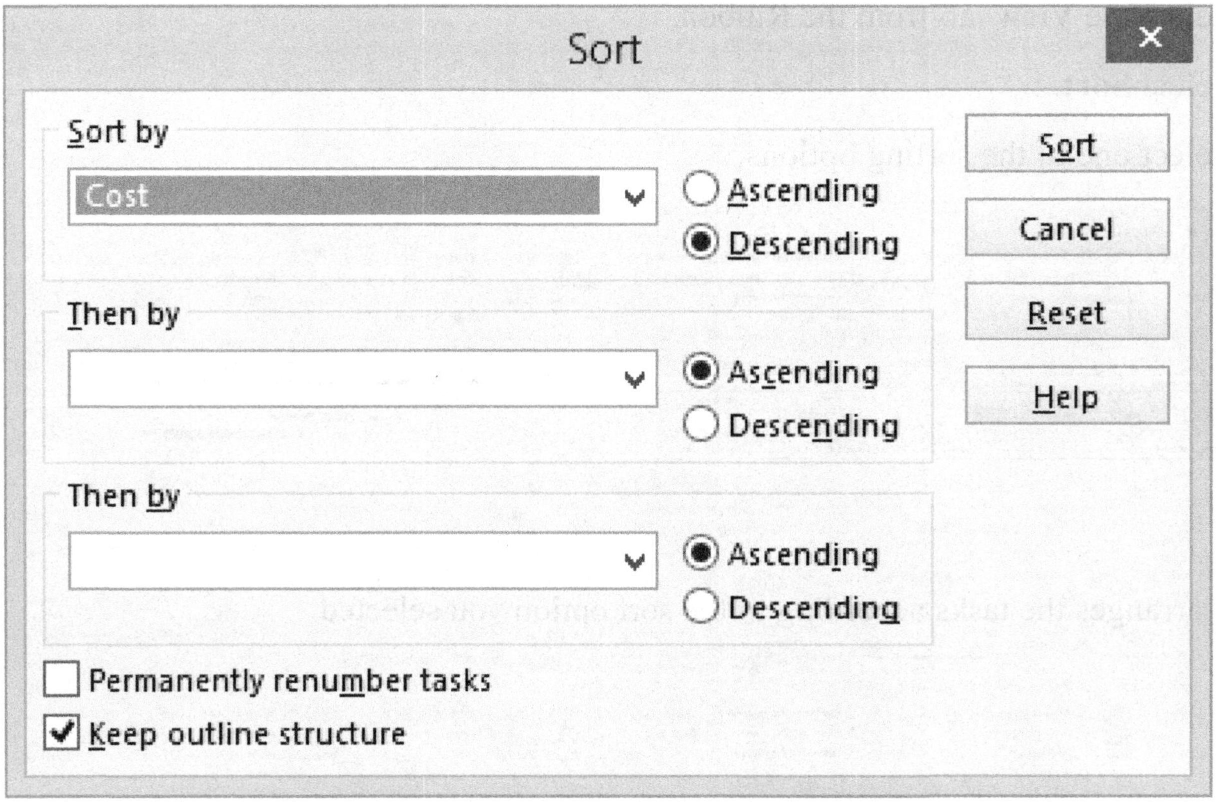


Step 1: Select an option from the first drop down list to indicate the first sorting option. Select **Ascending** or **Descending**.

Step 2: Select an option from the second drop down list to indicate the second sorting option. Select **Ascending** or **Descending**.

Step 3: Select an option from the third drop down list to indicate the third sorting option. Select **Ascending** or **Descending**.

Step 4: Check the **Permanently renumber tasks** box to change the task ID to the new sorting order.

Step 5: Check the **Keep outline structure box** to keep your current outline structure.

Step 6: Select **Sort**. To start over, select **Reset**. Or select **Cancel** to close the *Sort* dialog box without sorting.

## Grouping Information

Use the following procedure to group tasks.

Step 1: Select the **View** tab from the Ribbon.

Step 2: Select the **Group By** drop down list.

Step 3: Select one of the grouping options.

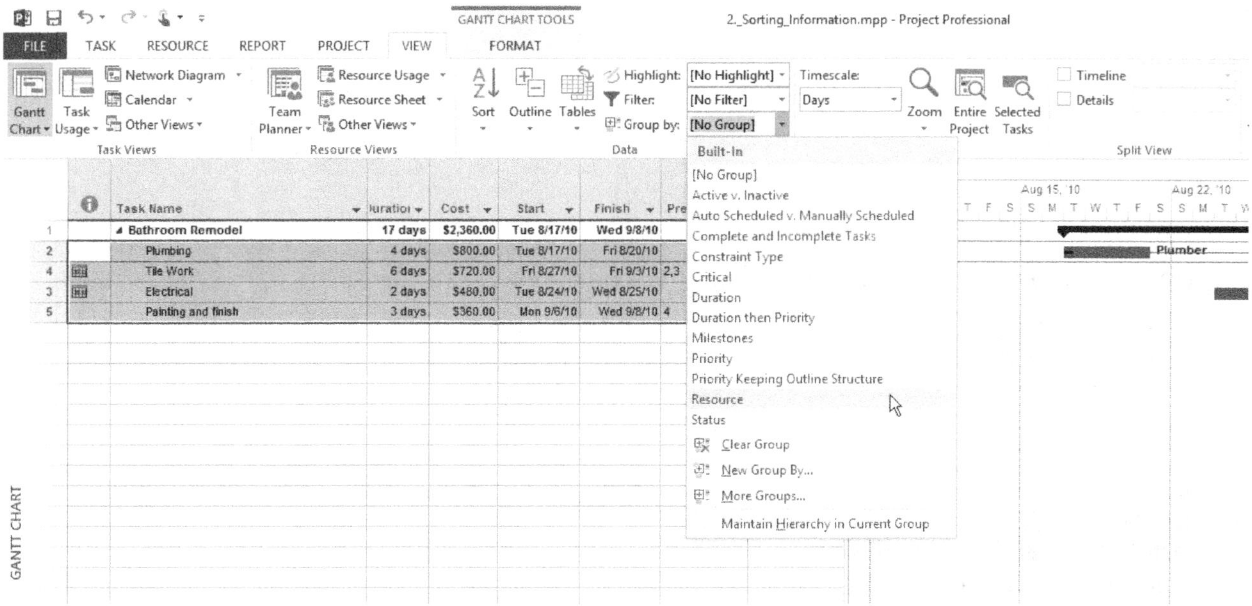

Project rearranges the tasks according to the grouping option you selected. It also displays a colored header for each group.

Accessing the *More Groups* dialog box.

Step 1: Select the **View** tab from the Ribbon.

Step 2: Select the **Group By** drop down list.

Step 3: Select **More Groups**.

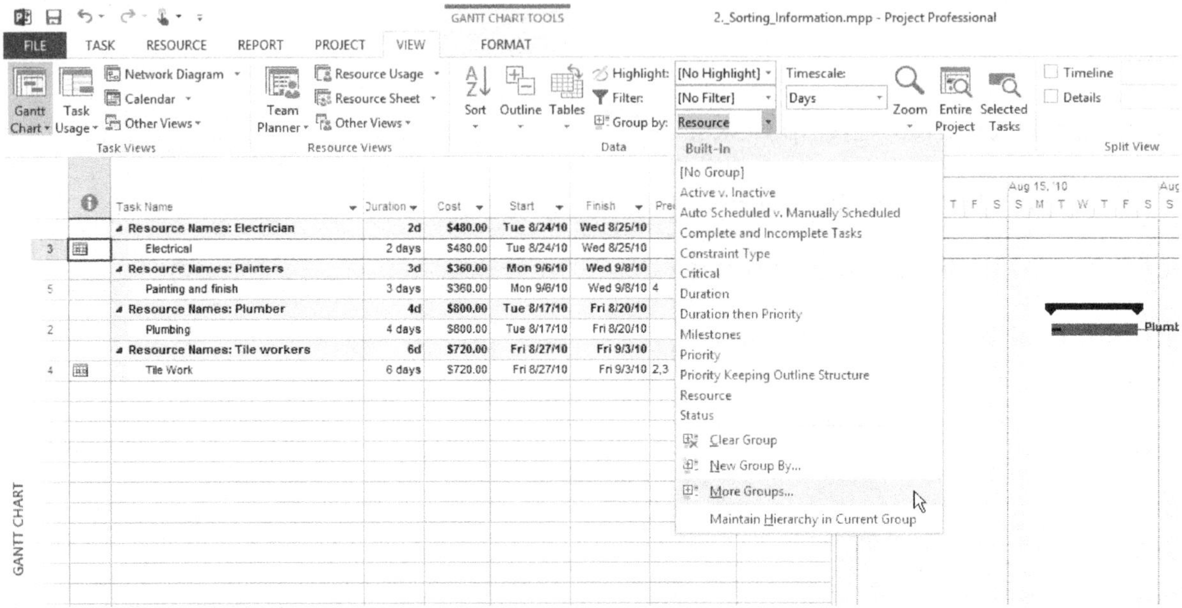


Project opens the *More Groups* dialog box.

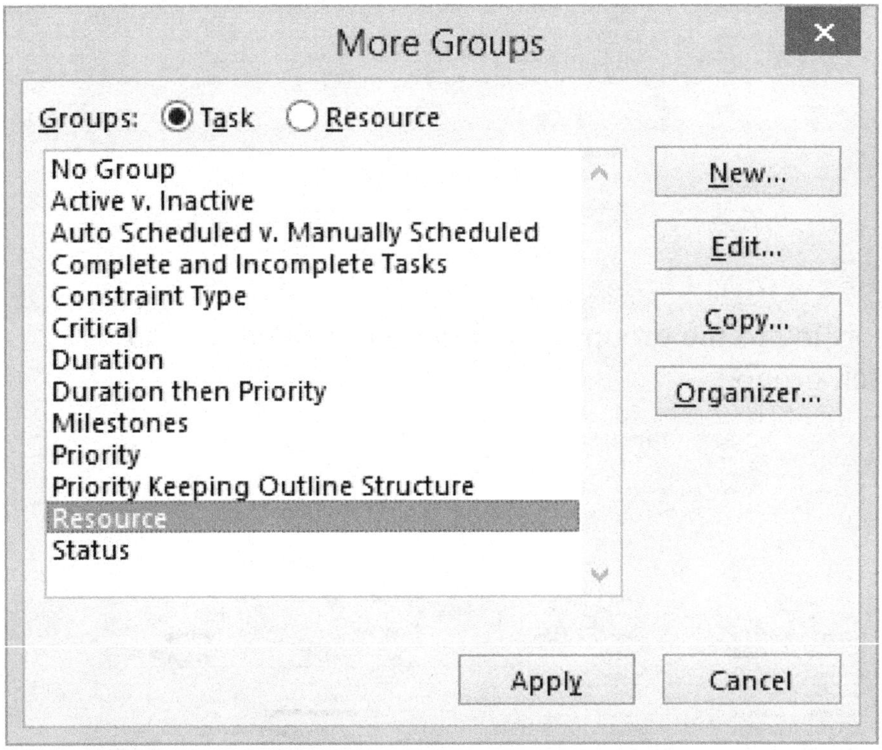


Step 4: Select either **Task** or **Resource** to narrow the list of groups.

Step 5: You can copy or create a new grouping by selecting **New** or **Copy**. You can edit a grouping by selecting **Edit**. These options open the *Group Definition* dialog box to allow you to define the grouping.

Step 6: Select a grouping from the list and select **Apply**. Or select **Cancel** to close the *More Groups* dialog box without applying a grouping.

The *Group Definition* dialog box.

Step 1: You can open the *Group Definition* dialog box by selecting **New**, **Edit,** or **Copy** from the *More Groups* dialog box. You can also select **Group by** from the **Project** menu and select **Customize Group By**.

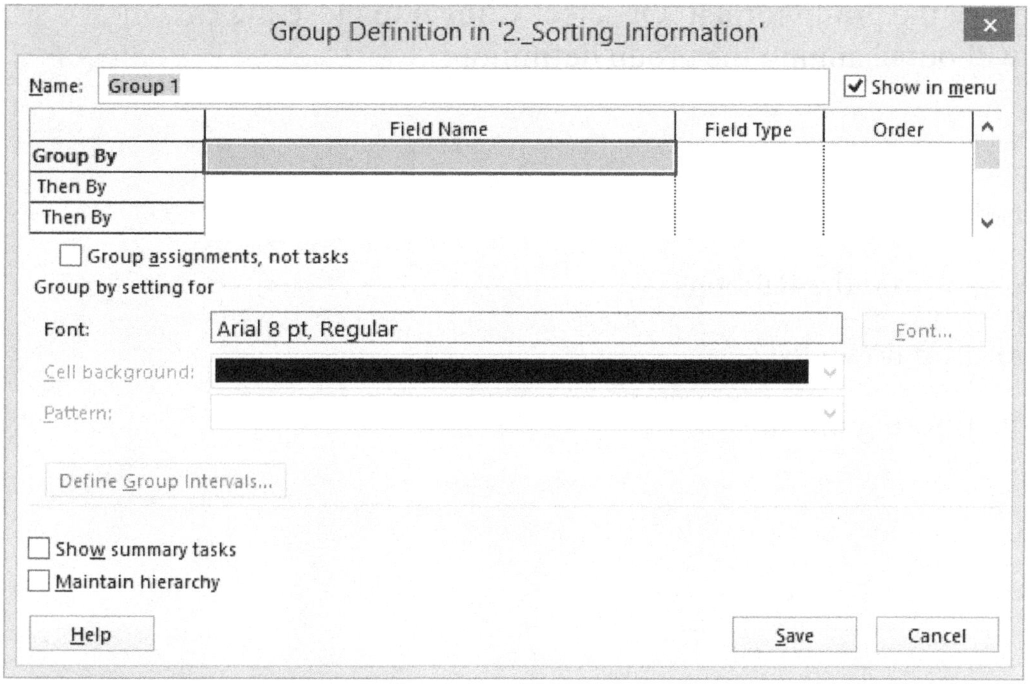


Step 2: The top area allows you to select multiple methods of grouping. For each level of grouping, select the following:

- Field Name
- Field Type
- Order

Step 3: The **Group assignments, not tasks** box allows you to group by assignments instead of tasks.

Step 4: The **Group By** settings area allows you to change the formatting for the group headings.

- Select the **Font** button to select a new font.

- Select a new **Cell background** from the drop down list.
- Select a **Pattern** for the cell background, if desired.

Step 5: The **Define Group Intervals** button allows you to define how groups are determined.

Step 6: Check the **Show summary tasks** box if you want to show the summary for each grouping.

Step 7: Check the **Maintain hierarchy** box to make sure your hierarchy is not changed with the grouping.

Step 8: Select **OK** to apply the group format. Or select **Cancel** to close the *Group Definition* dialog box without changing the group definition.

## Filtering Information

Use the following procedures to filter tasks.

Step 1: Select the **View** tab from the Ribbon.

Step 2: Select the **Filter** drop down list.

Step 3: Select one of the filtering options.

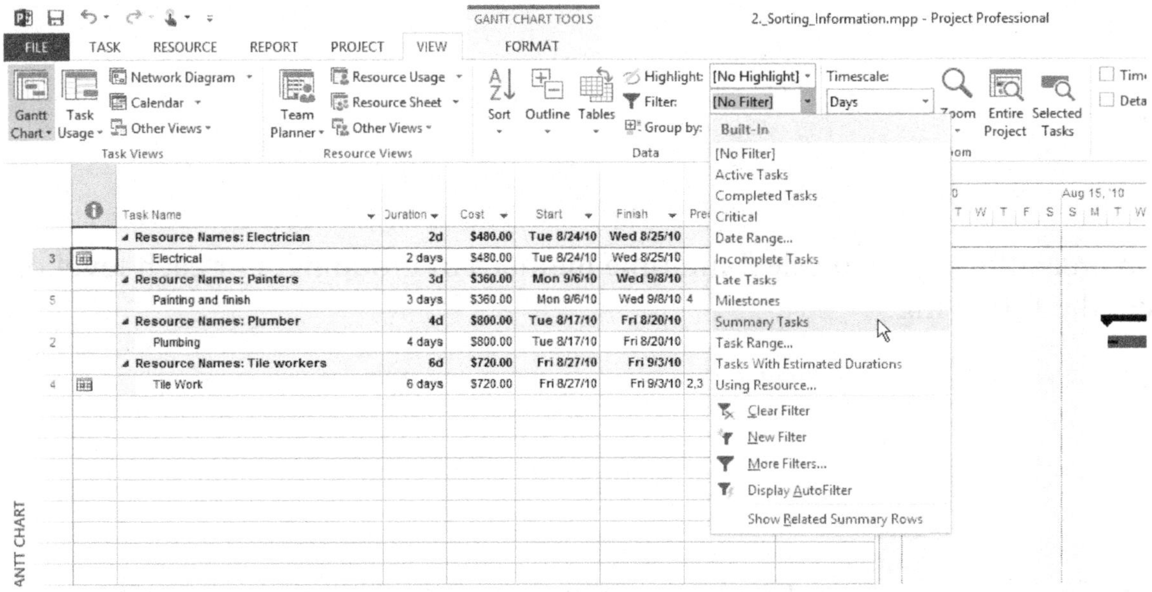


Step 4: Some filters require you to provide additional information. Select the required information and select **OK**.

Project only shows the tasks that meet the filter criteria.

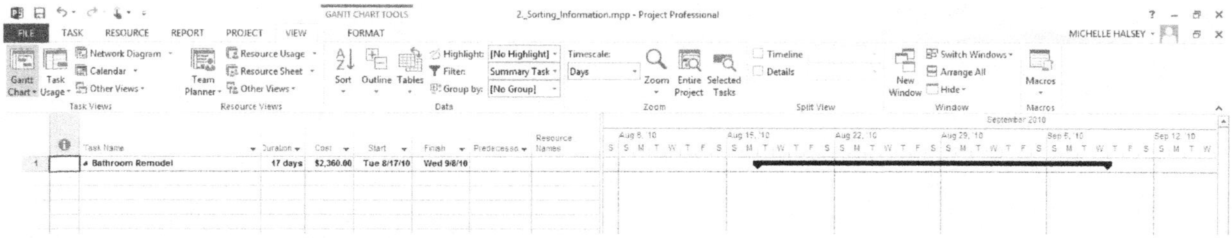

The *More Filters* dialog box.

Step 1: Select **Filtered For** from the **Project** menu. Select **More Filters**.

Project opens the *More Filters* dialog box.

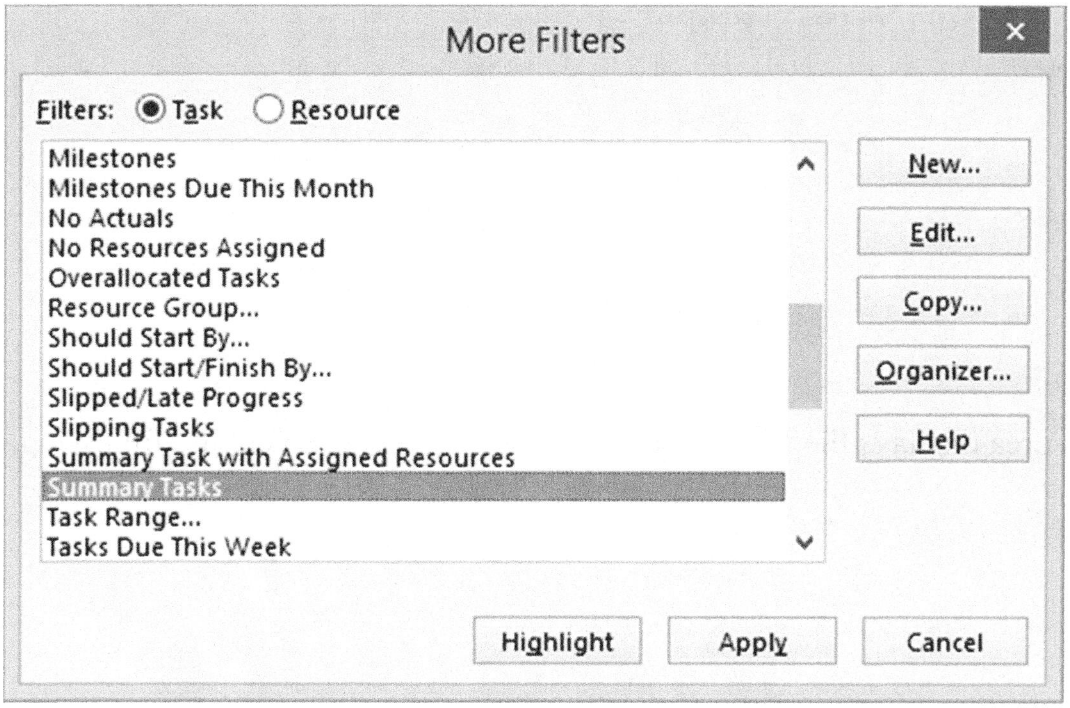


Step 2: Select either **Task** or **Resource** to narrow the list of filters.

Step 3: You can copy or create a new filter by selecting **New** or **Copy**. You can edit a filter by selecting **Edit**. These options open the *Filter Definition* dialog box to allow you to define the filter.

Step 4: Select a filter from the list and select **Apply**. Or select **Cancel** to close the *More Filters* dialog box without applying a filter.

The *Filter Definition* dialog box can be accessed by using the following procedure.

Step 1: You can open the *Filter Definition* dialog box by selecting **New**, **Edit,** or **Copy** from the *More Filters* dialog box.

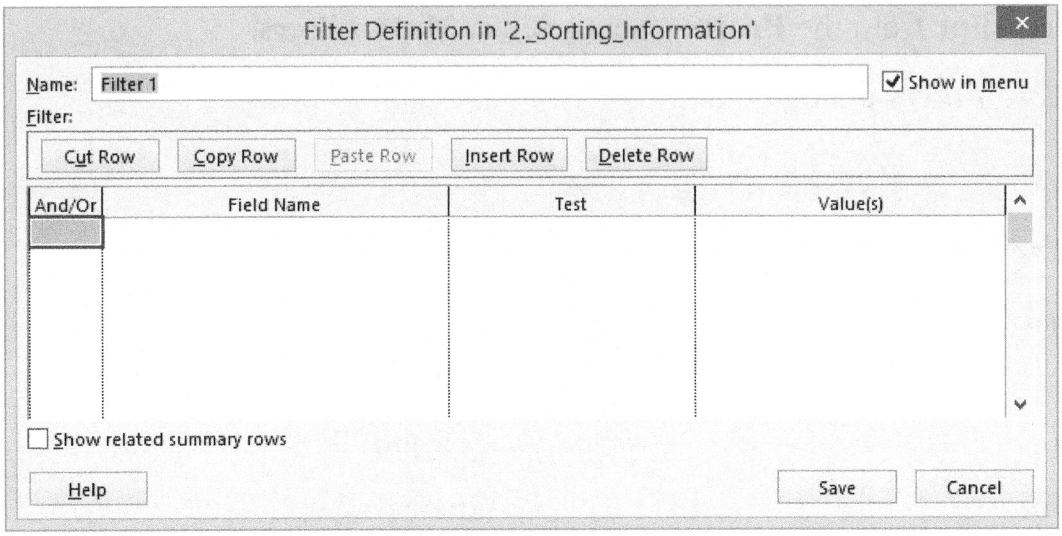


Step 2: The bottom area displays the filter definitions. For each line, select the following:

- And/Or
- Field Name
- Test
- Value

Step 3: Check the **Show Related summary tasks** box if you want to show the summary tasks.

Step 4: You can insert or delete rows, as well as cut, copy, or paste rows using the buttons above the filter definition rows.

Step 5: Select **OK** to apply the filter. Or select **Cancel** to close the *Filter Definition* dialog box without changing the filter definition.

## Using AutoFilters

Using the AutoFilter feature.

Step 1: Select the **View** tab from the Ribbon.

Step 2: Select the **Filter** drop down list.

Step 3: Select **Display AutoFilter**.

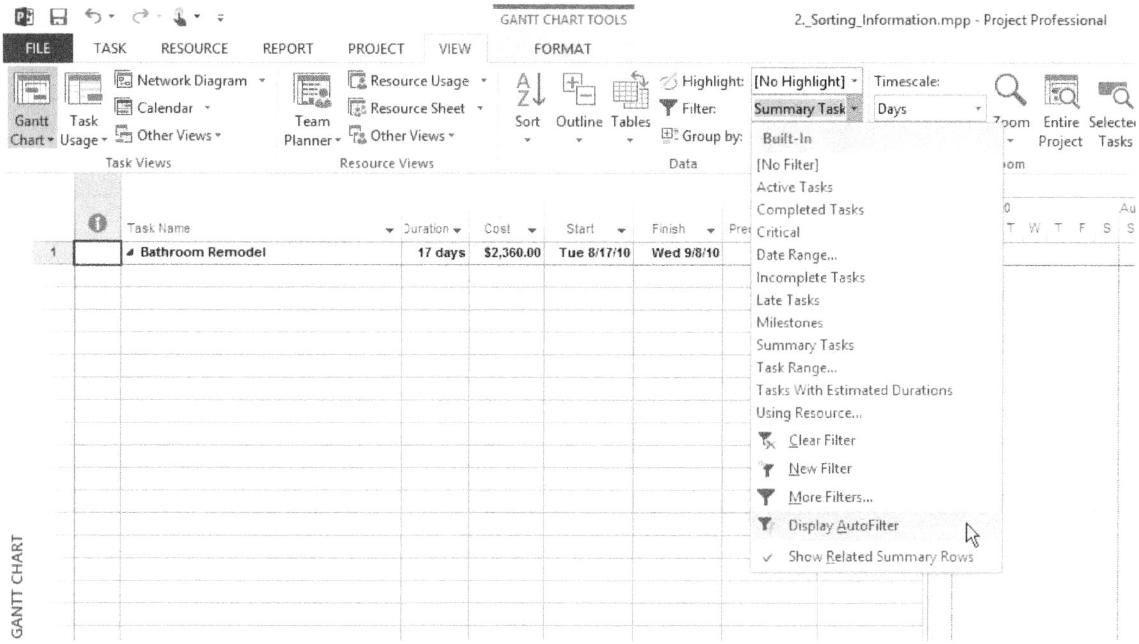


Project displays an arrow on the column headings.

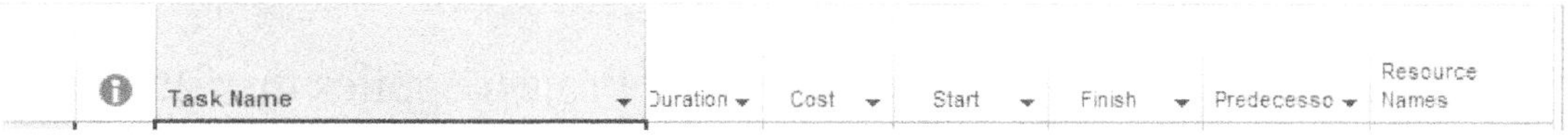

Step 4: Select the arrow next to the column you want to use for filtering to see the filtering options.

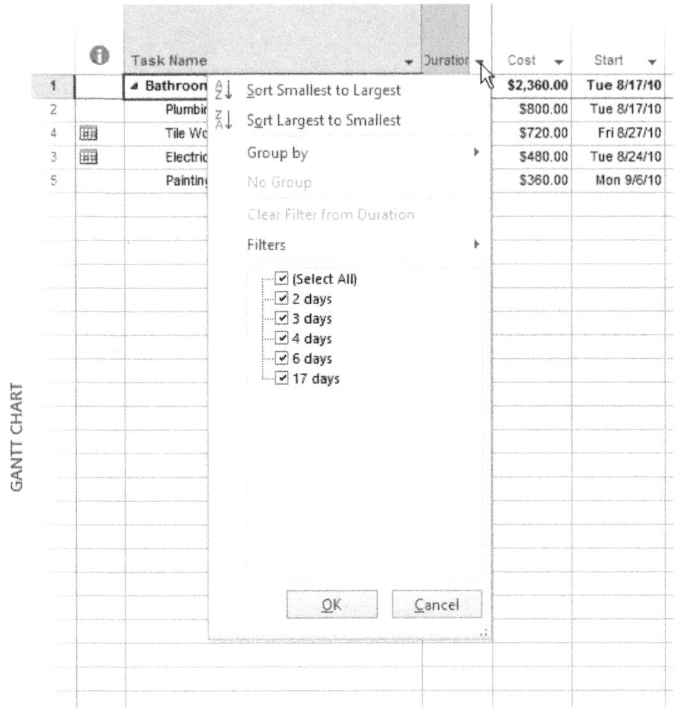

Step 5: Check the AutoFilter option(s) you want to display. Or check **Select All** to show all tasks.

Step 6: The AutoFilter menu includes custom options for grouping the filtered information. Select a group if desired.

Step 7: Select **OK**.

Step 8: Repeat with multiple column headings, if desired. Project applies the filters in the order you select them.

## Using Zoom

To open the Zoom dialog box, use the following procedure.

Step 1: Select **Zoom** from the **View** tab on the Ribbon.

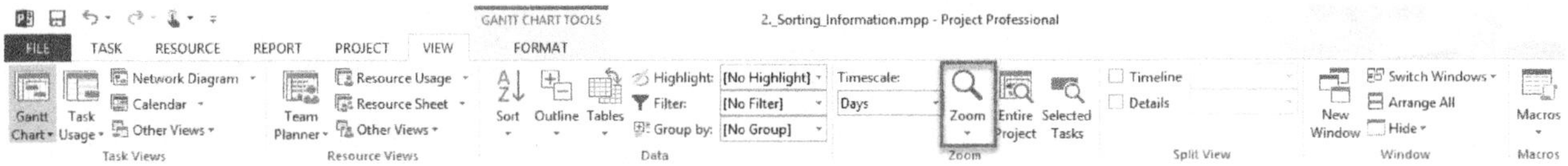

Step 2: Select **Zoom**.

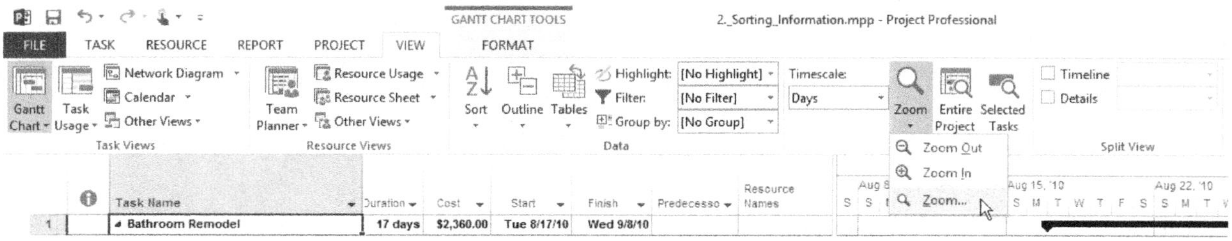


Project displays the *Zoom* dialog box.

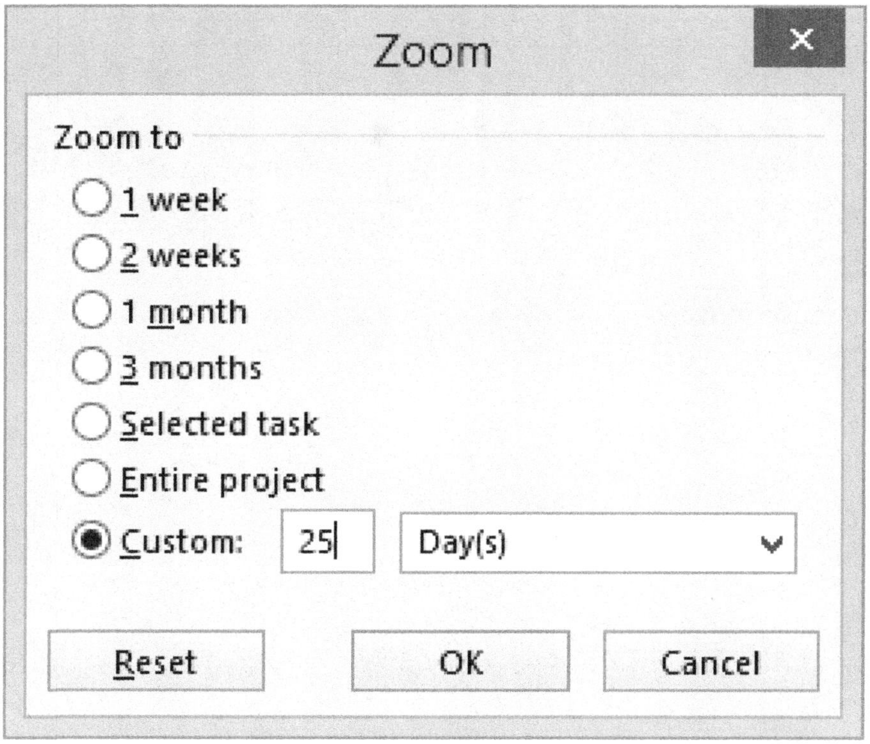


Step 3: Select a Zoom option. If you select Custom, enter the number and select the duration to indicate the custom zoom.

Step 4: Select **OK**. To start over, select **Reset**. To close the Zoom dialog box without changing the view, select **Cancel**.

## Chapter 3 – Working with Tasks

This chapter explains some of the more advanced features for working with tasks. You can overlap or delay tasks to shorten the project duration or adjust a schedule to allow for time between linked tasks. This chapter also explains how to set task deadlines and constraints. We will take a look at how to split tasks to accommodate a task interruption, such as when a resource is temporarily reassigned to another task. Finally, we will take a look at task types, task calendars, and task indicators.

### Overlapping Tasks

To add lead time, use the following procedure.

Step 1: Select the task you want to overlap. It should be a task that has a predecessor. Double-click to open the *Task Information* dialog box.

Step 2: Select the **Predecessors** tab.

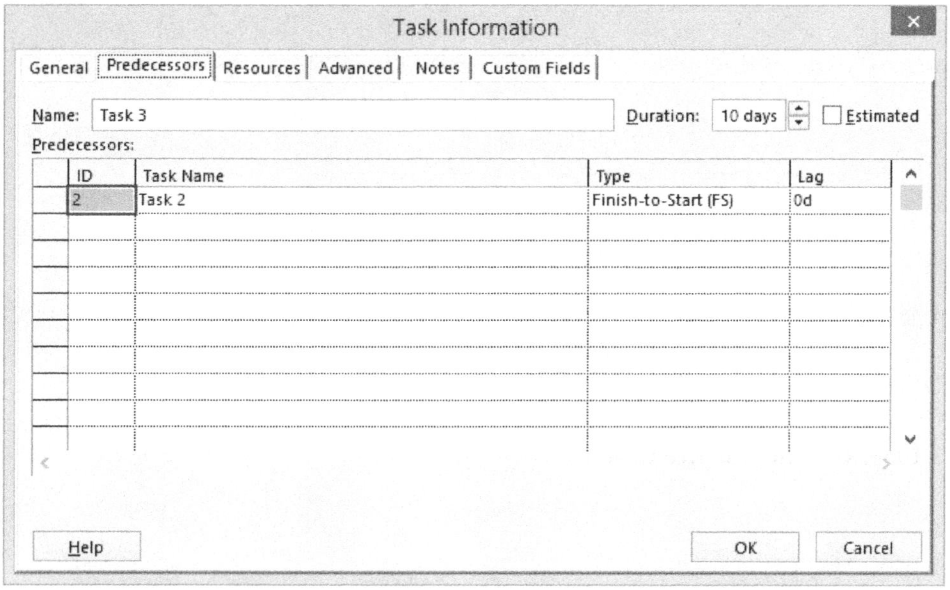


Step 3: In the **Lag** field, enter -50%.

Step 4: Select **OK** to close the *Task Information* dialog box.

Project displays the overlapping tasks on the Gantt chart.

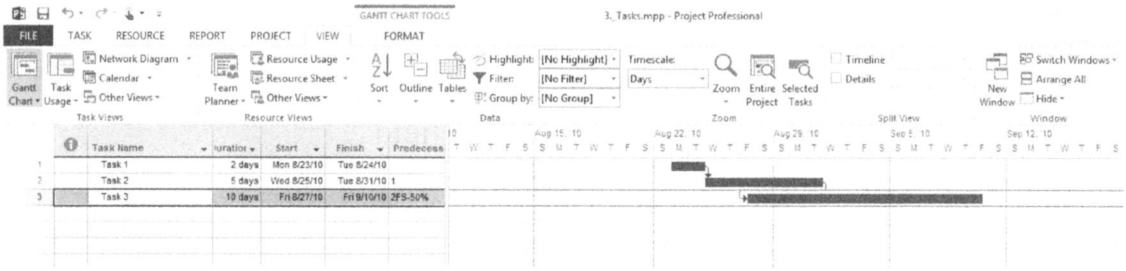

## Delaying Tasks

Use the following procedure to add lag time to a task.

Step 1: Select the task you want to delay. It should be a task that has a predecessor. Double-click to open the *Task Information* dialog box.

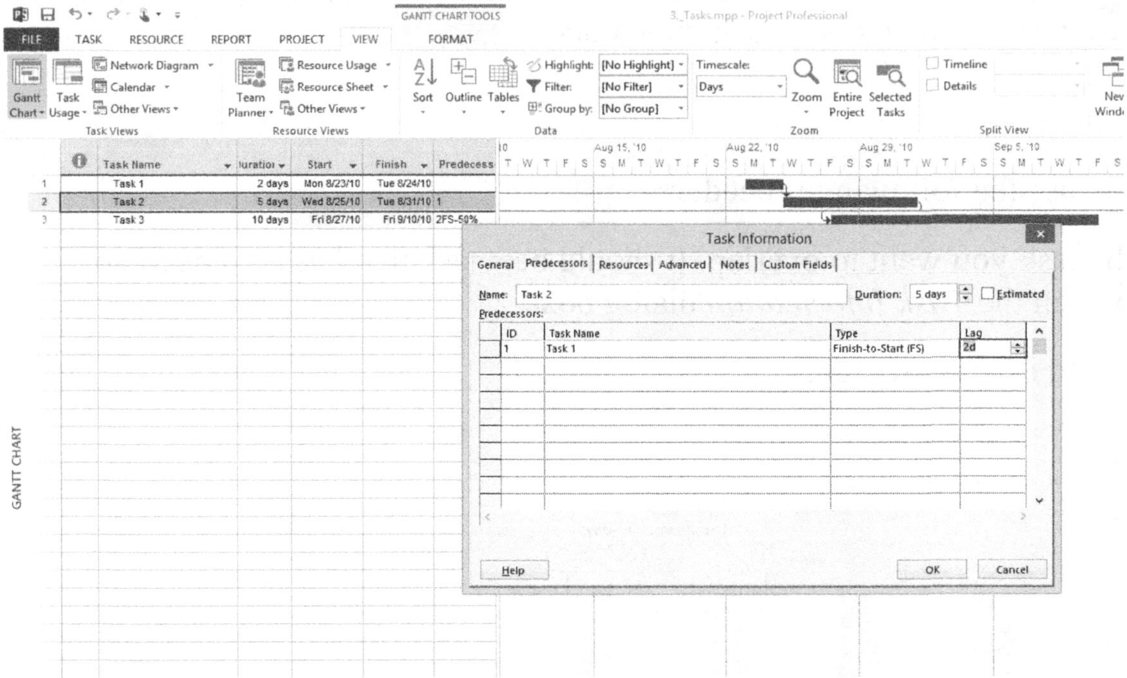


Step 2: In the **Lag** field, enter 2d.

Step 3: Select **OK** to close the *Task Information* dialog box.

Project displays the delayed task on the Gantt chart.

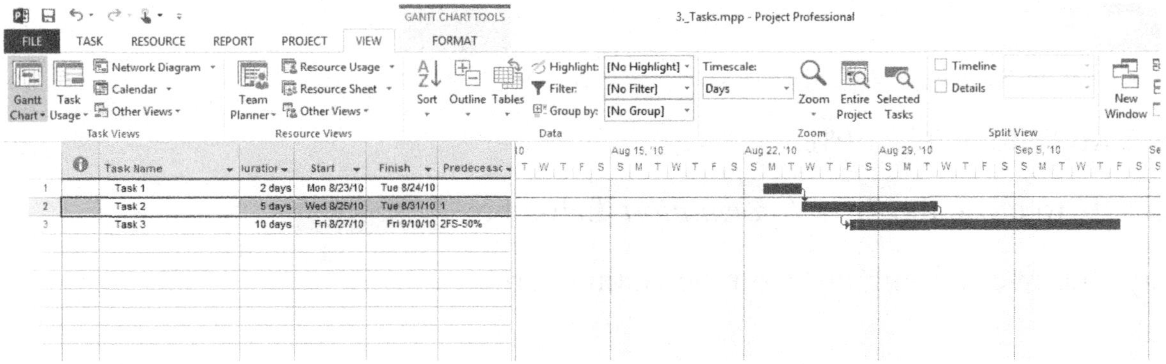


Notice the area shaded in yellow. The task for which Task 2 is a predecessor has changed, because of the delay. Also notice the Predecessors field.

## Setting Task Deadlines

To setup a deadline, use the following steps.

Step 1: Select the task for which you want to set a deadline. Double-click to open the *Task Information* dialog box.

Step 2: Select the **Advanced** Tab.

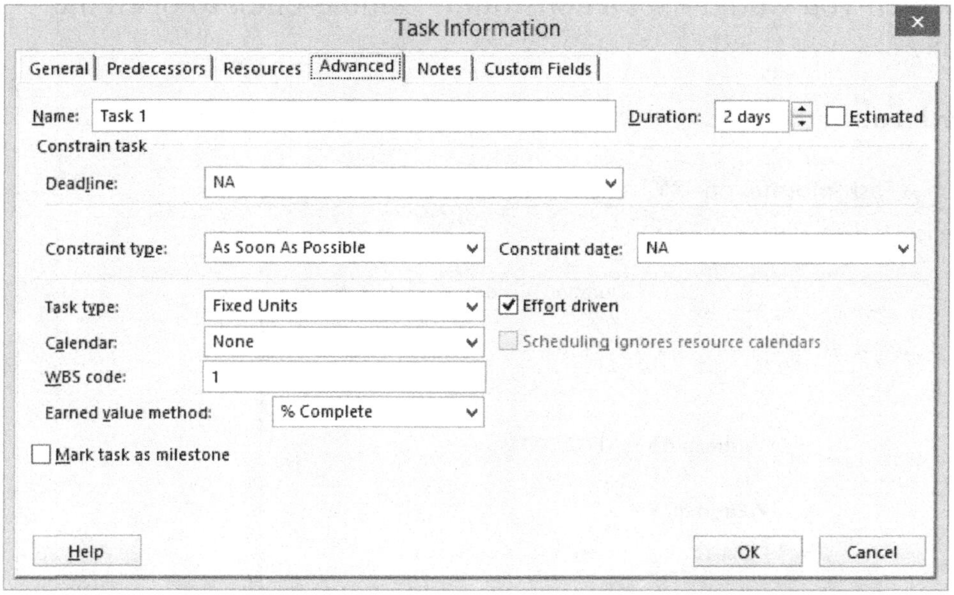


Step 3: In the **Deadline** field, click the down arrow and select the deadline from the calendar.

Step 4: Select **OK** to close the *Task Information* dialog box.

The following example shows a task whose deadline has passed, and the work has not yet been shown complete, so the **Indicator** column displays a warning.

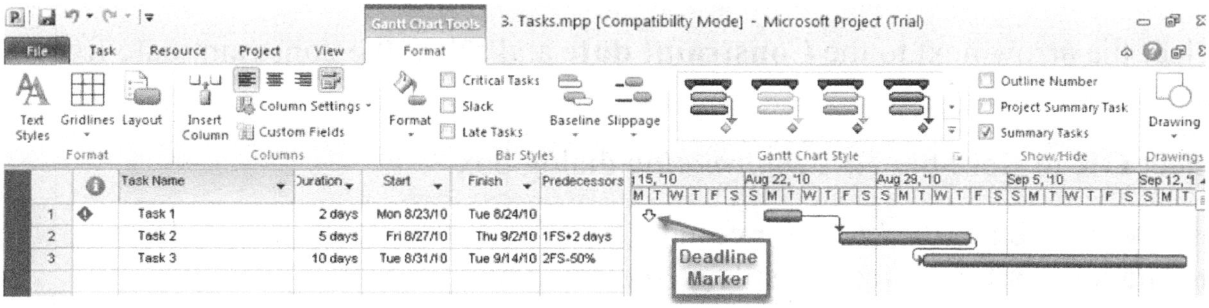


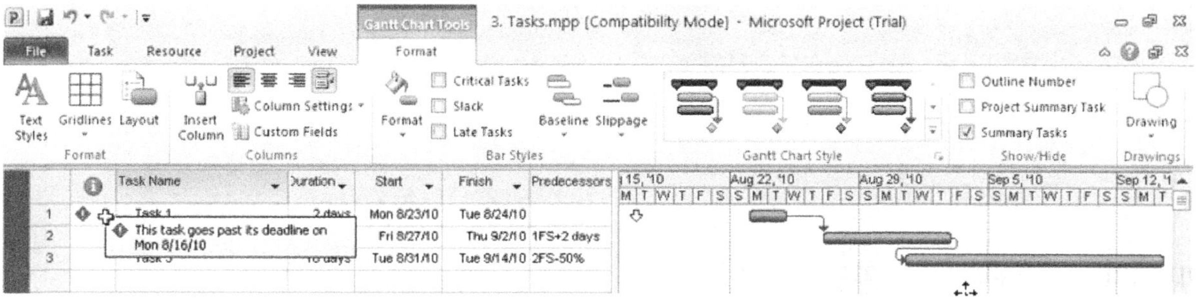

## Setting Task Constraints

Use the following procedure to set a constraint type and date.

Step 1: Select the task for which you want to set a constraint. Double-click to open the *Task Information* dialog box.

Step 2: Select the **Advanced** Tab.

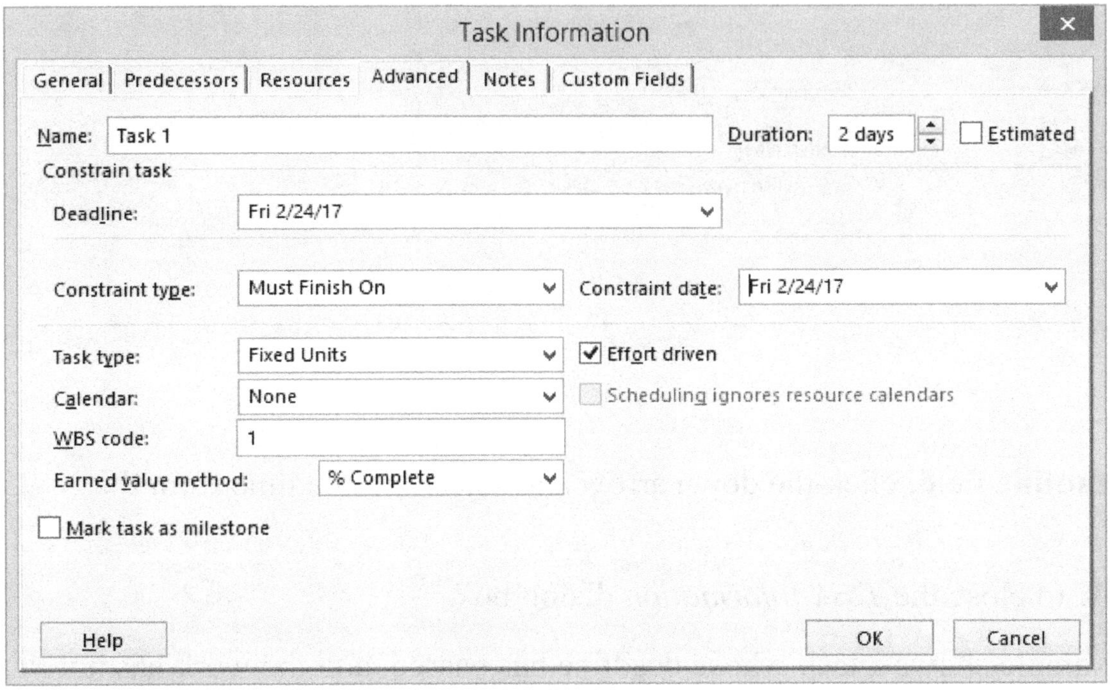


Step 3: Select the **Constraint type** from the drop down list.

Step 4: Select the arrow next to the **Constraint date** and select the constraint date from the calendar.

Step 5: Select **OK** to close the *Task Information* dialog box.

Project displays an icon in the Indicator column to indicate that the task includes a constraint. The text for the indicator explains the constraint.

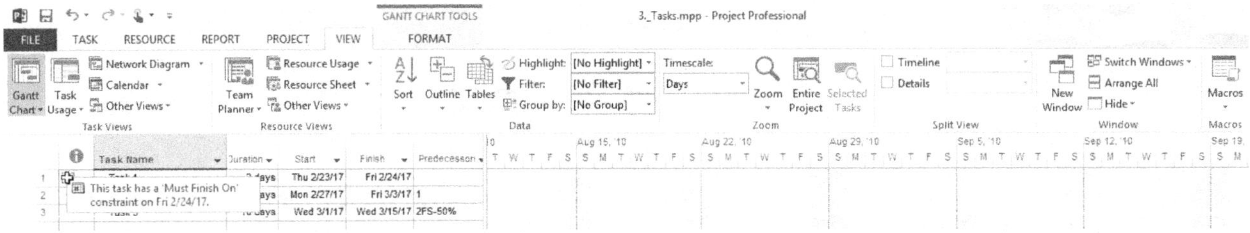


How to open the Constraint Dates table.

Step 1: Select the **View** tab from the Ribbon.

Step 2: Select the **Tables** drop down list.

Step 3: Select **More Tables**.

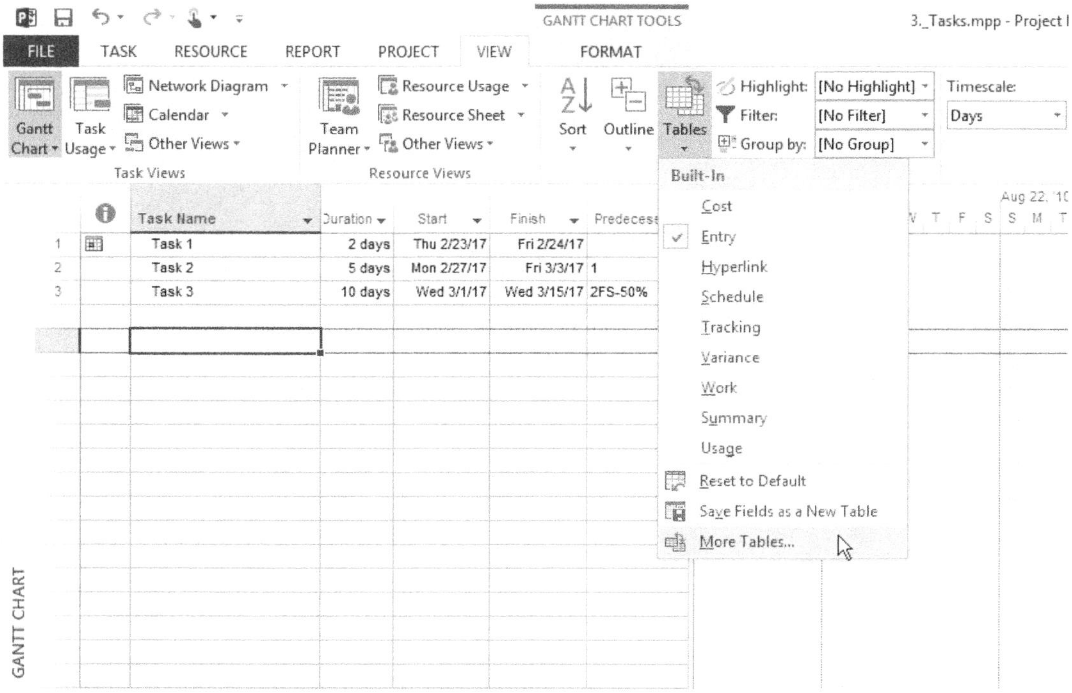


Step 4: Select **Constraint Dates**.

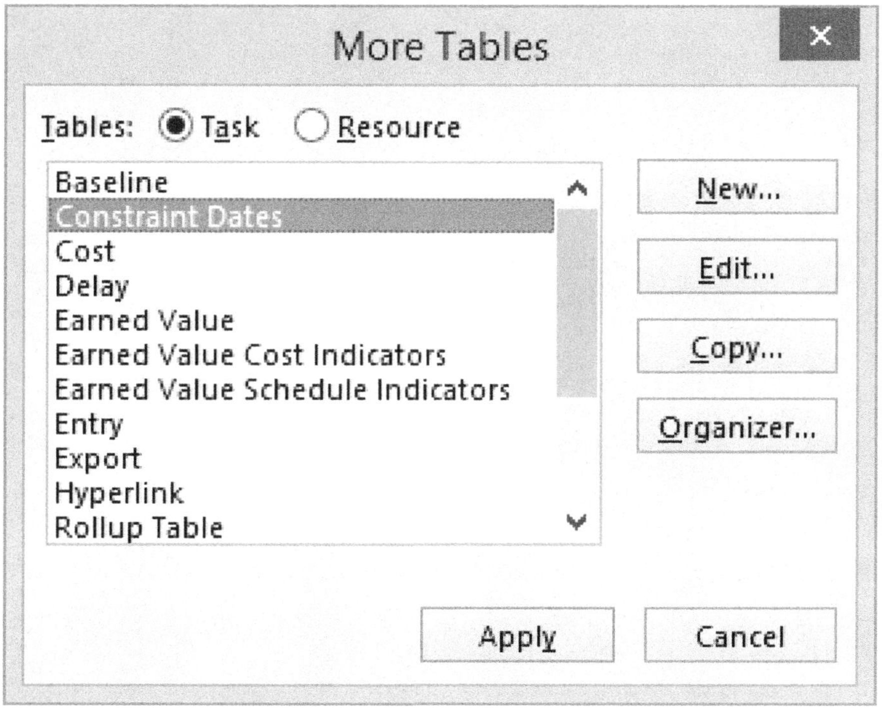


Step 5: Select **Apply**.

Project displays the Constraint Dates table in the left side of the window. The Gantt chart is still displayed on the right side of the window, allowing you to easily refer to the schedule while setting constraints for multiple tasks.

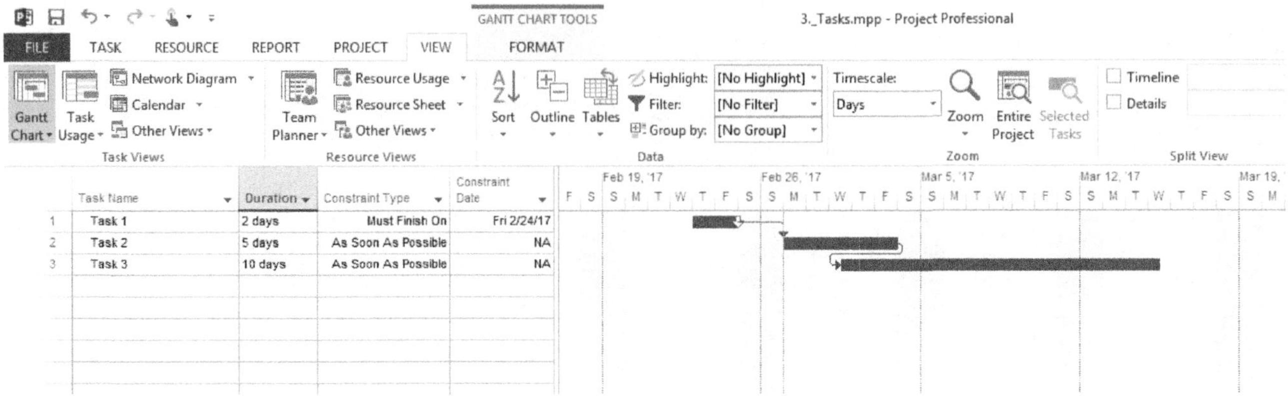

## Splitting Tasks

Use the following procedure to split up tasks.

Step 1: Select the task you want to split.

Step 2: Select the **Split Tasks** tool from the Task tab on the Ribbon.

Project displays the *Split Tasks* dialog.

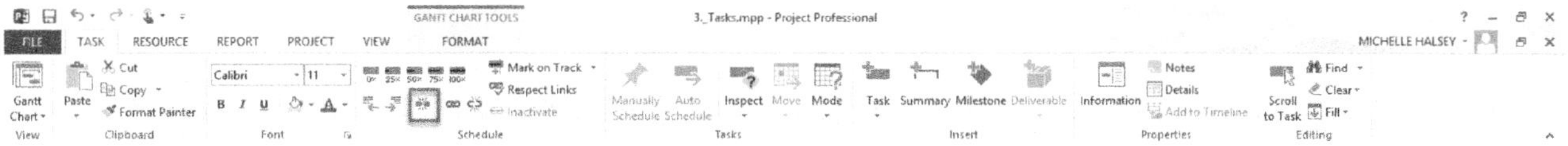


Step 3: Hover your mouse over the task and Project displays the corresponding date in the Split Tasks dialog.

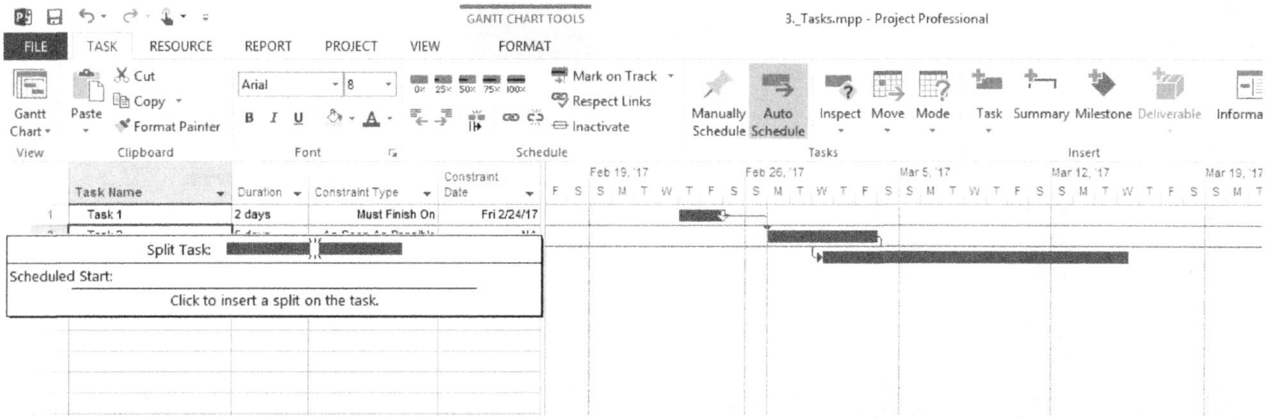


Step 4: When the date corresponds to the date where you need to split the task, click the mouse.

Project inserts a break in the task, as illustrated below.

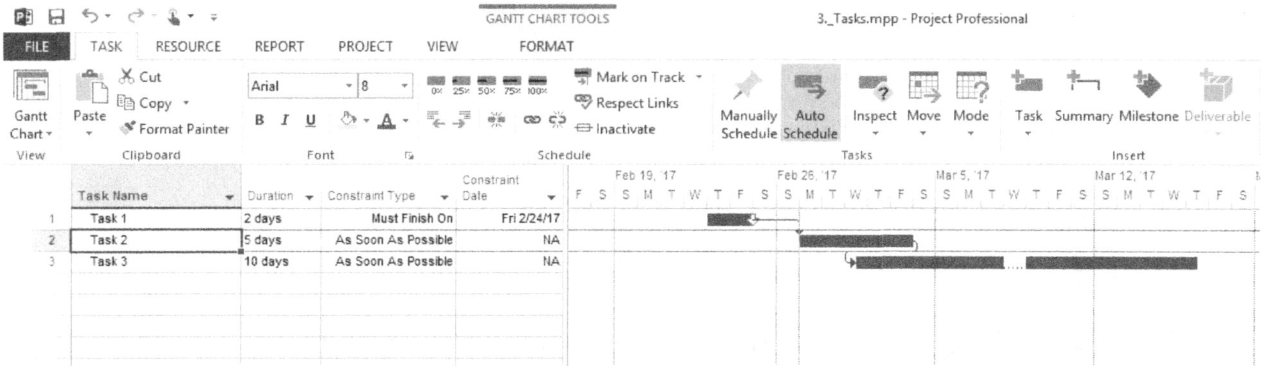

Step 5: You can drag the second part of the task to any start date.

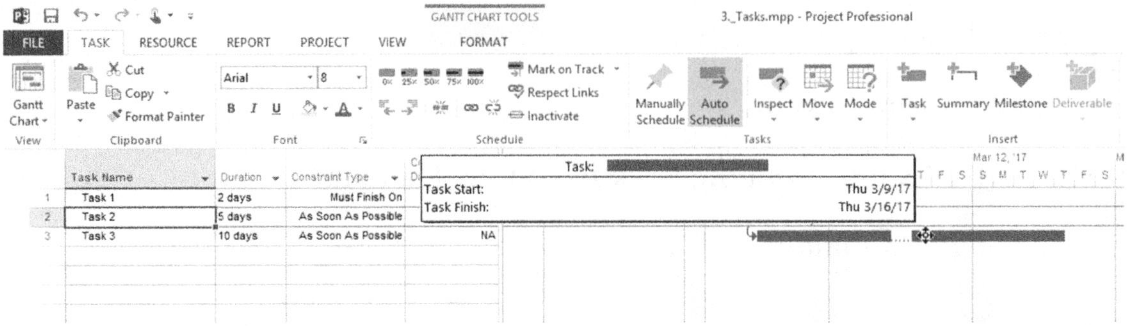


The following illustration shows a task that has been split, and then resumed on the following Monday.

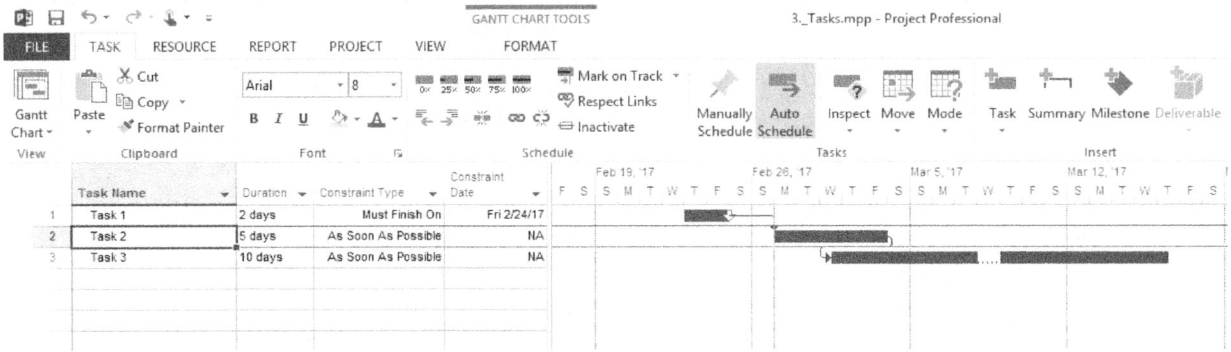


## Understanding Task Type

There are three types of tasks that affect scheduling in a project. Project recalculates any changes made differently, based on which type of task you select. Let's look at a fixed unit task first.

### Fixed Unit Task

When you make revisions to a fixed unit task, Project makes the recalculations as follows:

- Revisions to units creates a recalculated duration.
- Revisions to duration creates a recalculated work value.
- Revisions to the work value creates a recalculated duration.

Let's look at an example to show how this works. Open the sample file *4. Tasks 2.mpp*. The sample task has a duration of 10 days for one full-time resource. Project calculates the work to be 80 hours.

Imagine that another full-time resource is now available to help with the task. Assign the second resource, and see the new duration of 5 days.

Use the following procedure.

Step 1: Double-click the Fixed Unit Task to open the *Task Information* dialog box.

Step 2: Select the **Resources** tab.

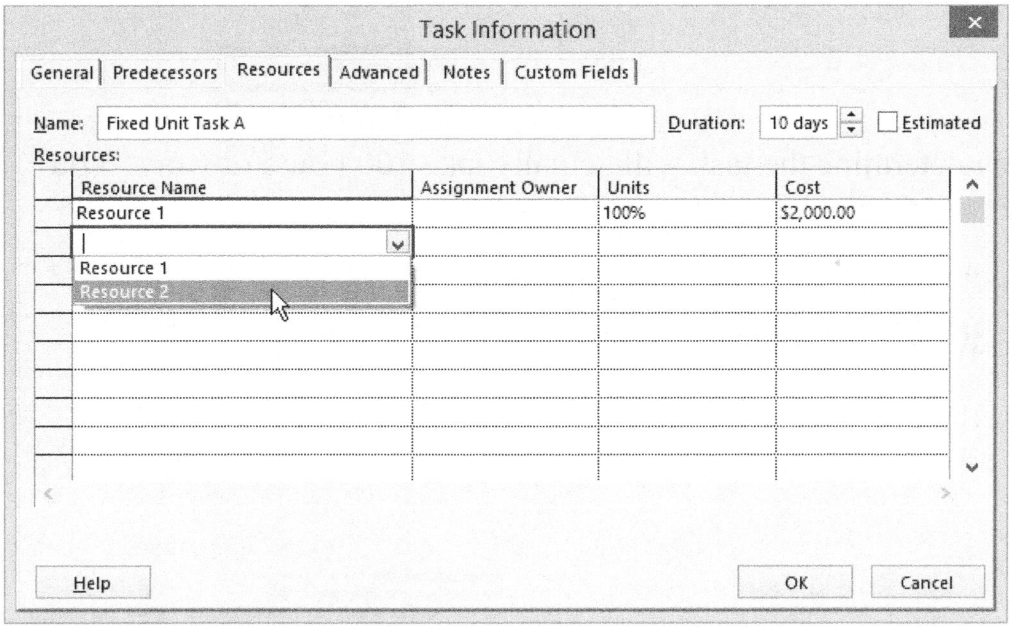


Step 3: Select the down arrow under **Resource Name** and select Resource 2.

Step 4: Select **OK** to close the *Task Information* dialog box.

Project recalculates the duration. Now the task only takes 5 days.

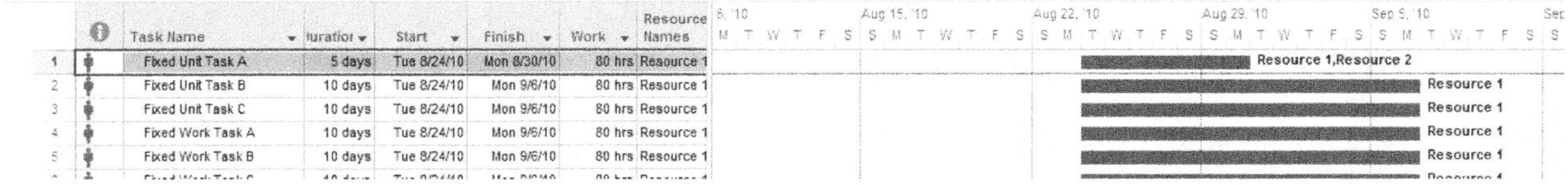


Now imagine that you must complete the task in eight days. Change the duration and see the recalculated work value.

Use the following procedure.

Step 1: Enter 8 as the duration for Fixed Unit Task B.

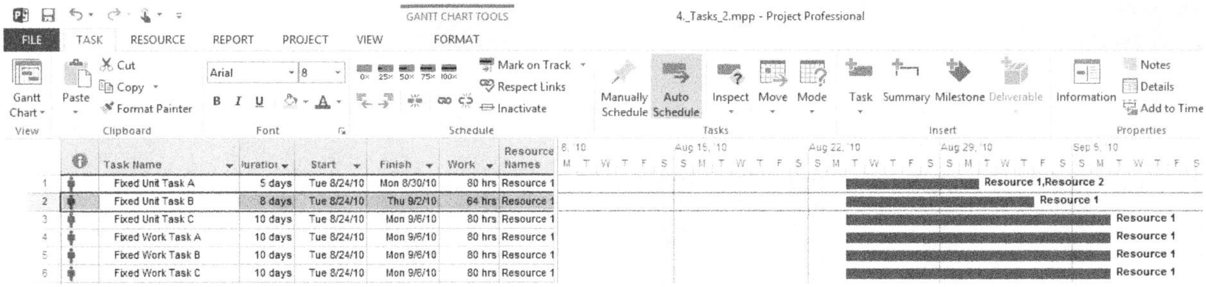

Project recalculates the Work.

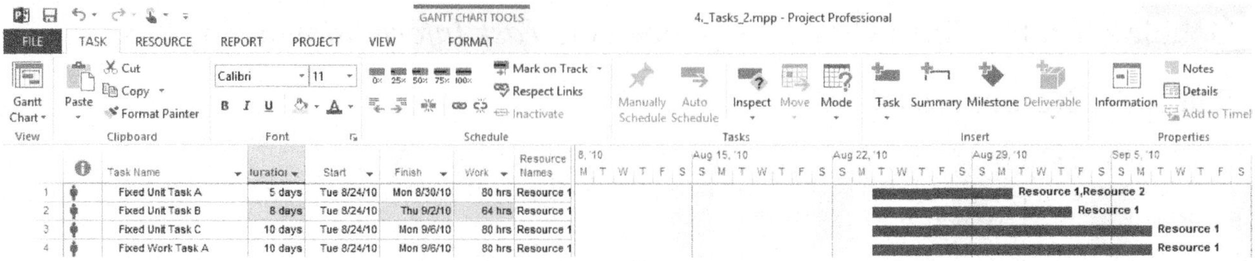


Finally, imagine that you determine the task will actually take 100 hours of work. You change the work and see the recalculated duration.

Use the following procedure.

Step 1: Enter 100 as the Work for Fixed Unit Task C.

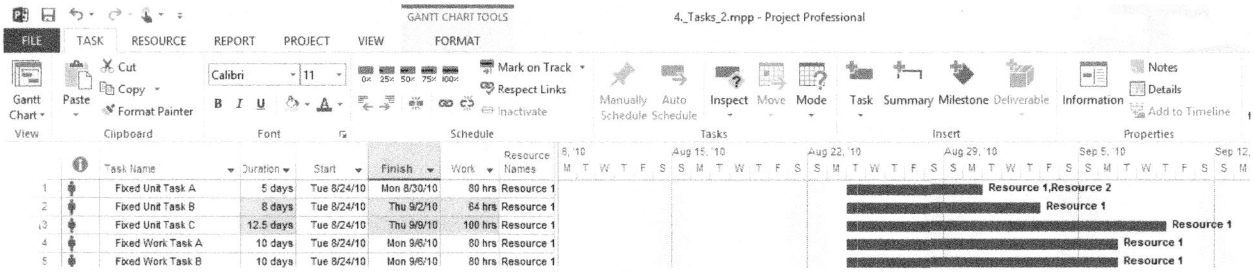


Project recalculates the duration.

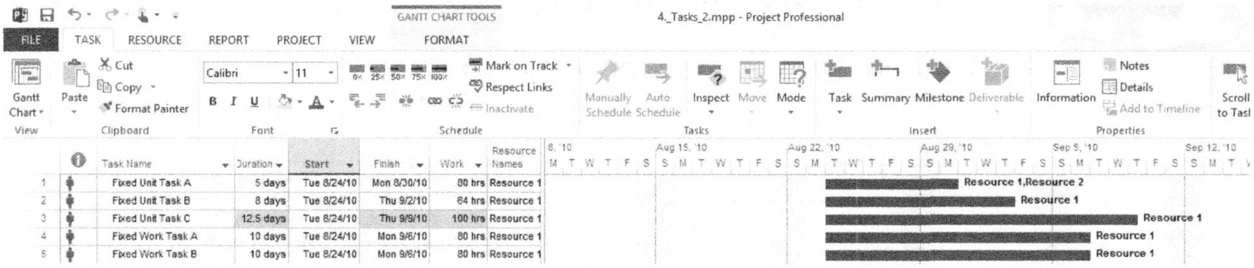


## Fixed Work Task

When you make revisions to a fixed work task, Project makes the recalculations as follows:

- Revisions to units creates a recalculated duration.
- Revisions to duration recalculates units.
- Revisions to the work value creates a recalculated duration.

The sample task is the same as the previous example, except the task type is **Fixed work**.

Imagine that another full-time resource is now available to help with the task. For Fixed Work Task A, assign the second resource, and see the new duration of 5 days. Use the procedure in the previous example to change the resource.

Project recalculates the duration. Now the task only takes 5 days.

Now imagine that you must complete the task in eight days. For Fixed Work Task B, change the duration and see the recalculated work value. Use the procedure in the previous example to change the duration.

Project recalculates the resource units. Resource 1 is now overallocated.

Finally, imagine that you determine the task will actually take 100 hours of work. For Fixed Work Task C, change the work and see the recalculated duration. Use the procedure in the previous example to change the work.

Project recalculates the duration.

**Fixed Duration Task**

When you make revisions to a fixed duration task, Project makes the recalculations as follows:

- Revisions to units creates a recalculated work value.
- Revisions to duration creates a recalculated work value.
- Revisions to the work value recalculates the resource units.

The sample task is the same as the previous example, except the task type is **Fixed duration**.

Imagine that another full-time resource is now available to help with the task. For Fixed Duration Task A, assign the second resource. Project has reallocated each resource to 50%, making each resource available to work on other tasks 50% of the time for the duration of the task. Use the procedure in the previous example to change the resource.

Project recalculates the duration. The duration has not changed. The work has not changed. However, now each resource is allocated at 50%.

Now imagine that you must complete the task in eight days. For Fixed Duration Task B, change the duration and see the recalculated work value. Use the procedure in the previous example to change the duration.

Project recalculates the work. Notice that the work value is 64 hours.

Finally, imagine that you determine the task will actually take 100 hours of work. For Fixed Duration Task C, change the work. The resource is now over allocated. Use the procedure in the previous example to change the work.

## Assigning a Task Calendar

Use the following procedure to create a new calendar specific to a task

Step 1: Select the **Project** tab from the Ribbon.

Step 2: Select **Change Working Time**.

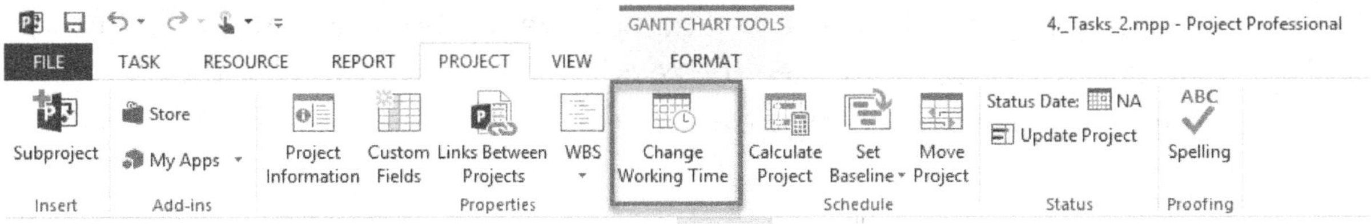


Step 3: Select **Create New Calendar**.

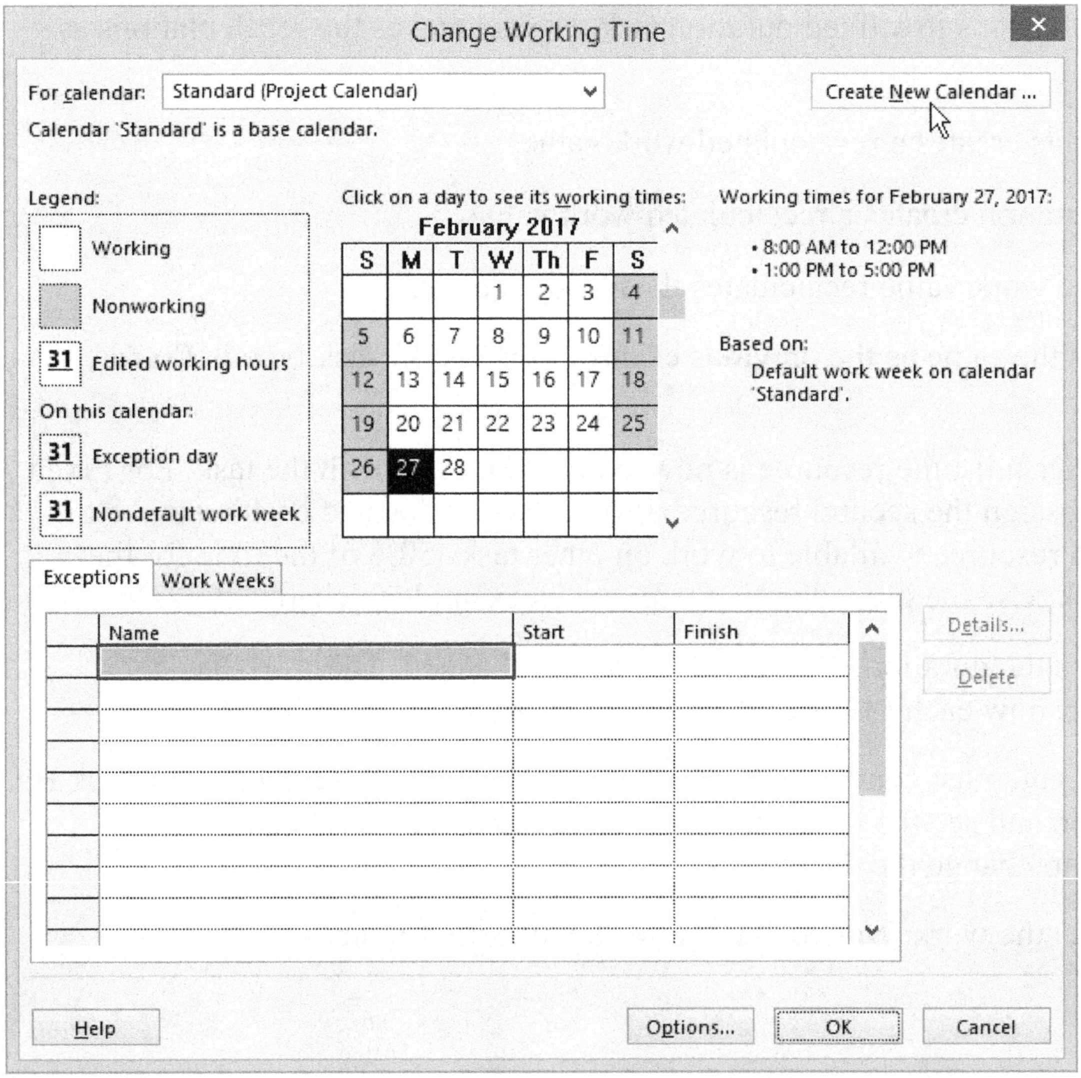

Project displays the *Create New Base Calendar* dialog box.

Step 4: Enter a name for the calendar.

Step 5: Select an option for the starting point for the base calendar and select **OK**.

Step 6: In the *Change Working Time* dialog box, select the **Work Weeks** tab.

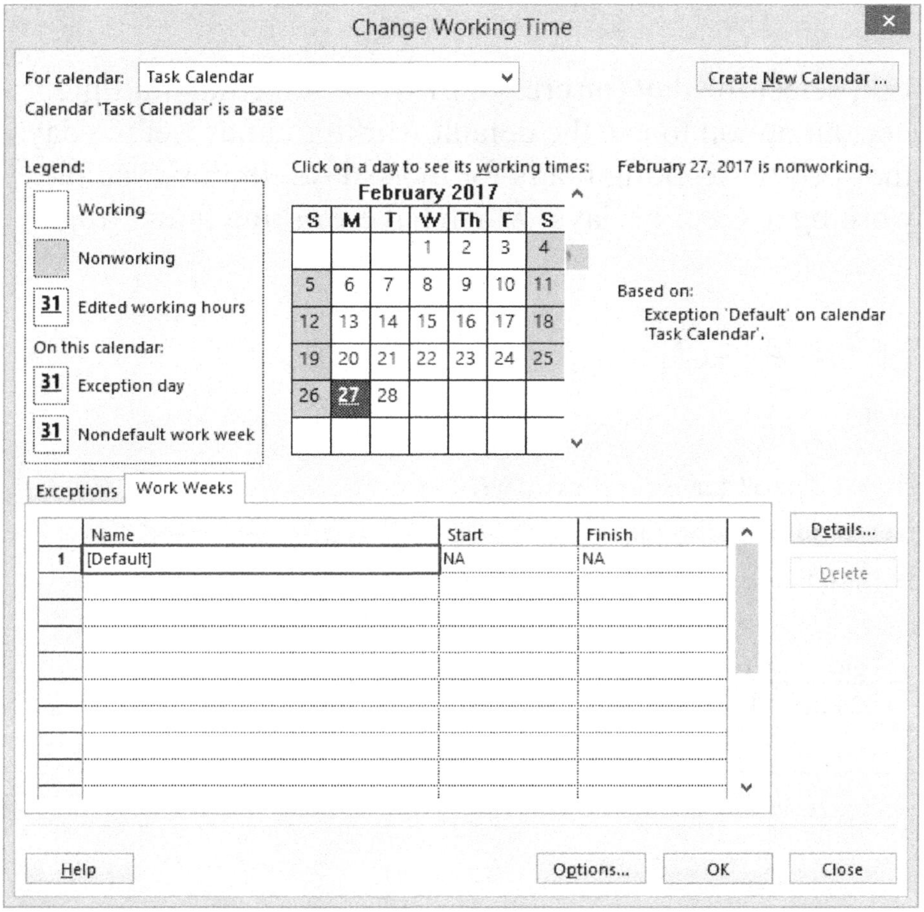

Step 7: Select **Details** to set the work week.

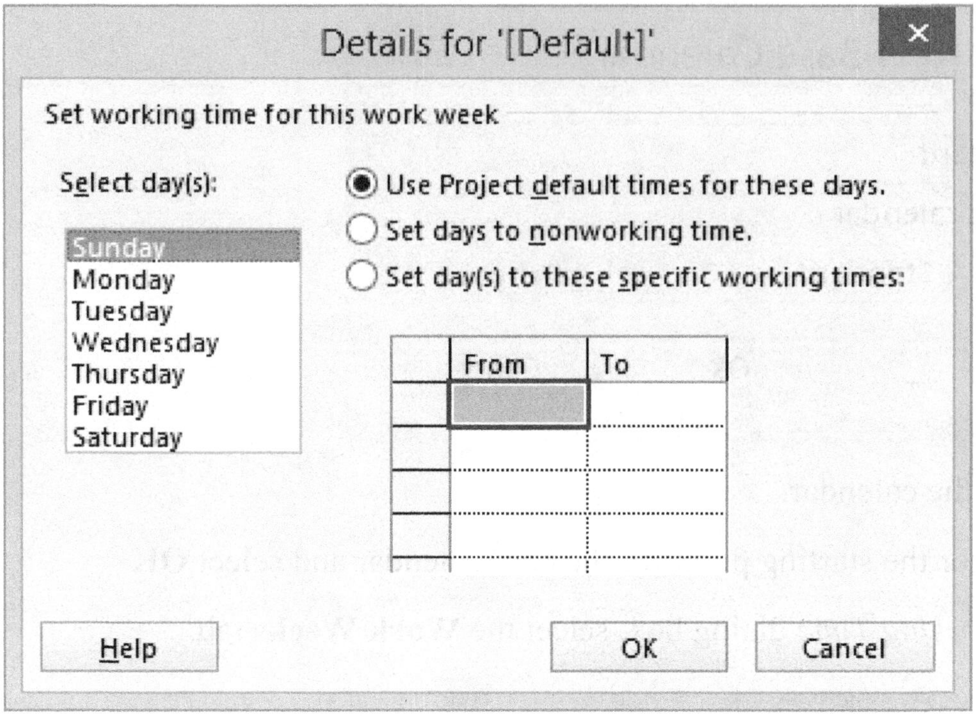


Step 8: For each day of the week, select the day (or press Ctrl while selecting multiple days that are the same) and select an option to use the default working times, set the days to nonworking time, or enter the specific working hours for those days. In this example, we will set everything to nonworking, except Fridays, which have working hours from 4pm to 12 am.

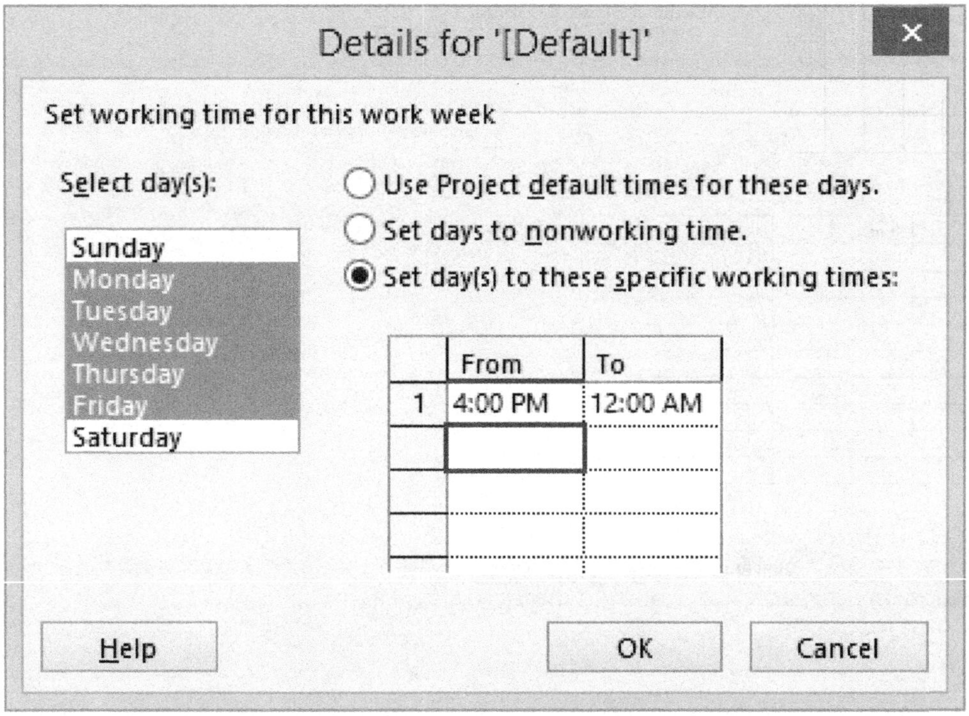

Step 9: Select **OK** to close the *Details* dialog box. Select **OK** to close the *Change Working Time* dialog box.

## Applying the New Calendar to a Task

Step 1: Select the task for which you want to set a task calendar. Double-click to open the *Task Information* dialog box.

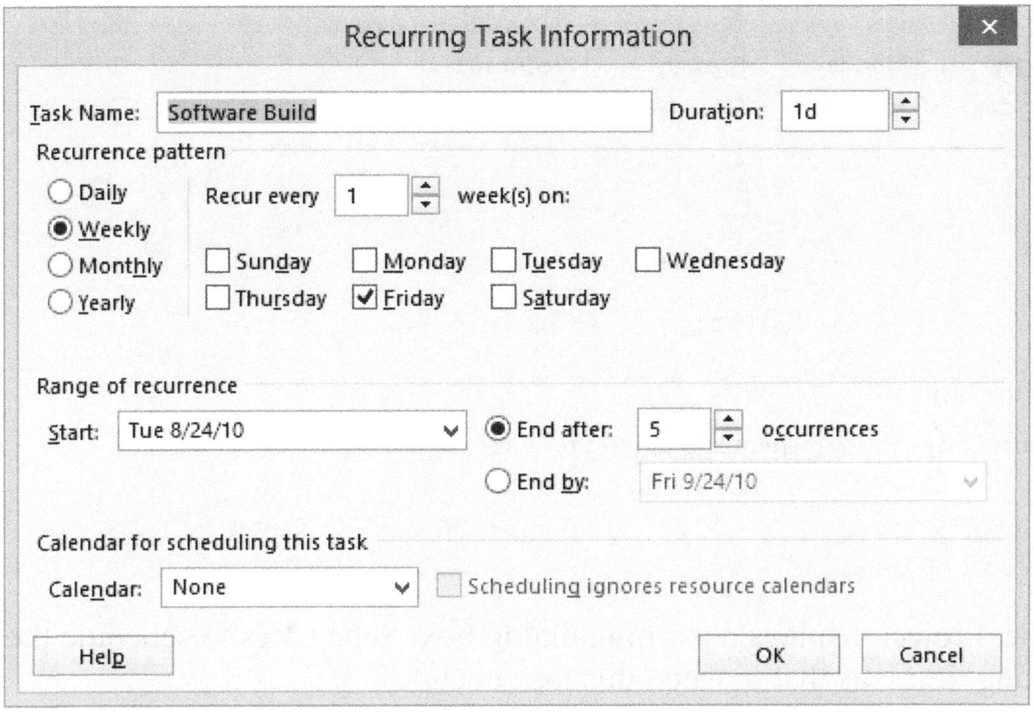


Step 2: Select the calendar you created from the **Calendar** drop down list.

Step 3: Check the **Scheduling ignore resource calendars**, if applicable.

Step 4: Select **OK**.

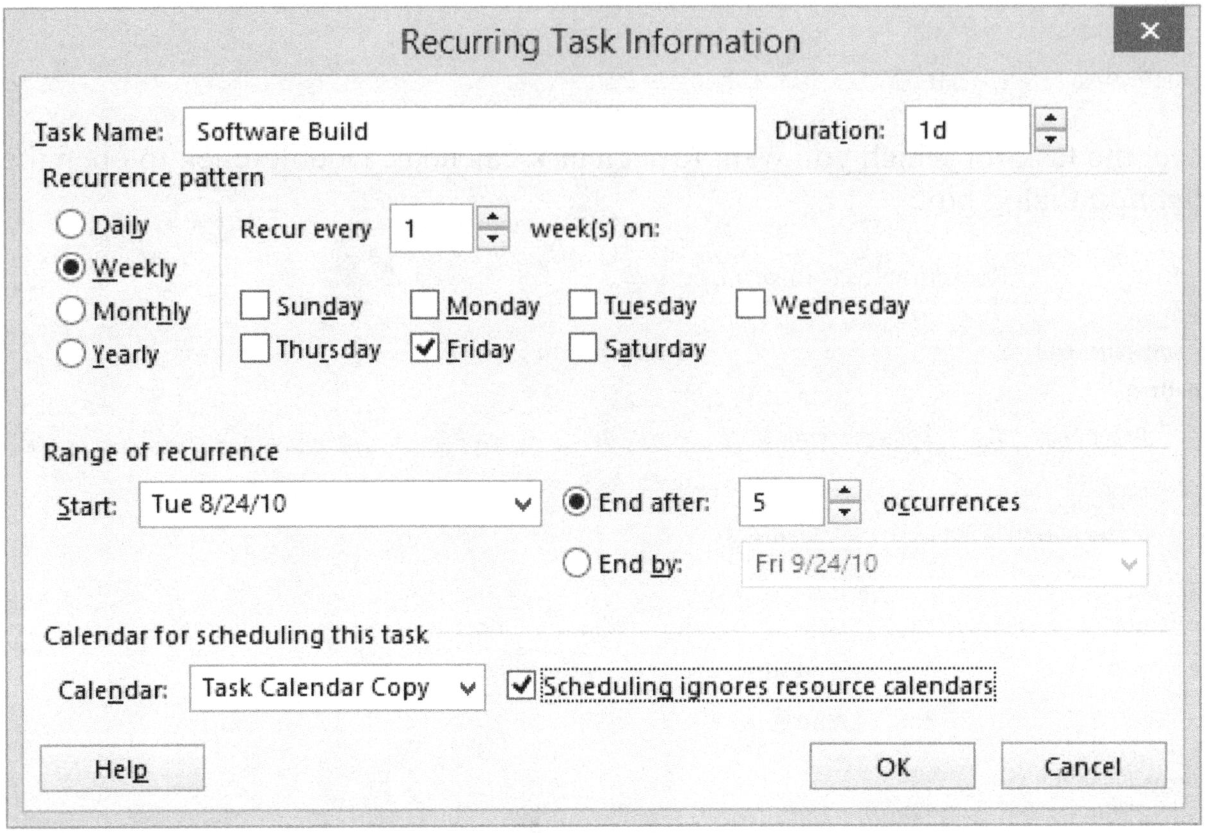


Step 5: In this example, Project displays a warning dialog box. Select **Yes** to schedule the tasks during nonworking times, as that is when this task occurs.

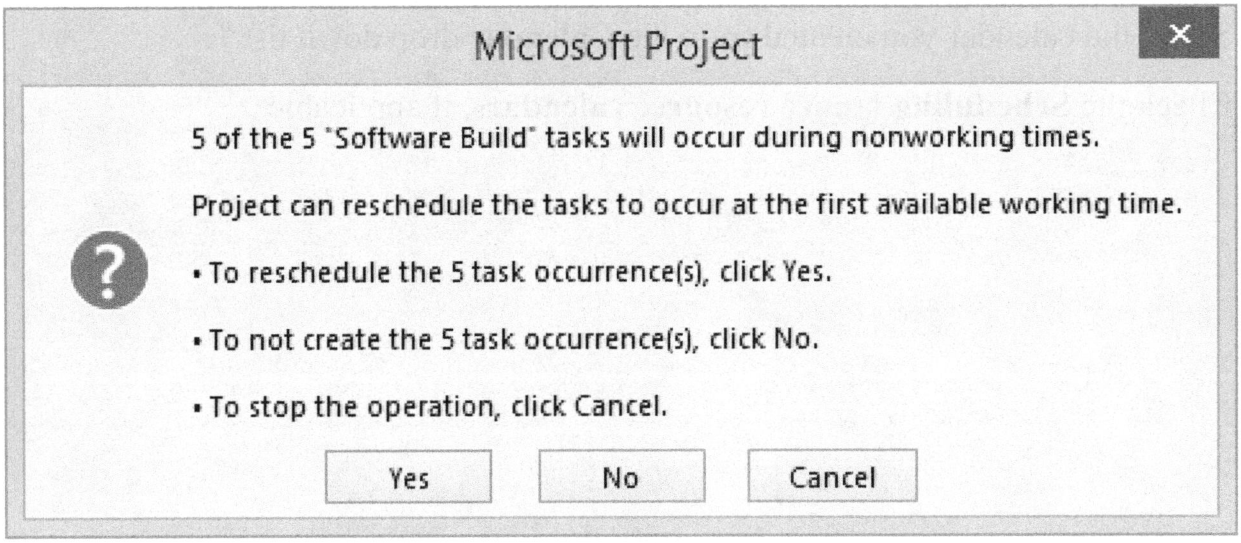

Notice the new duration and task indicators.

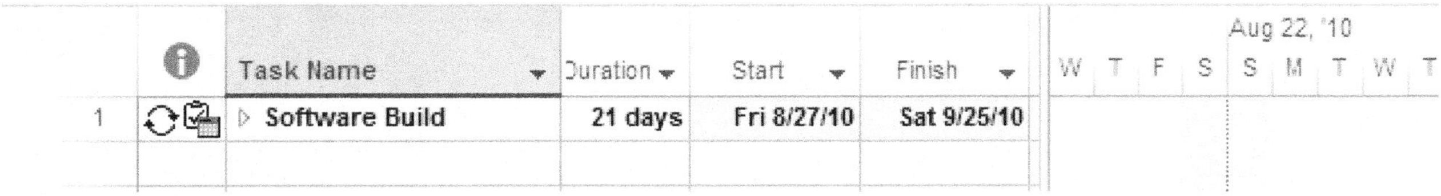


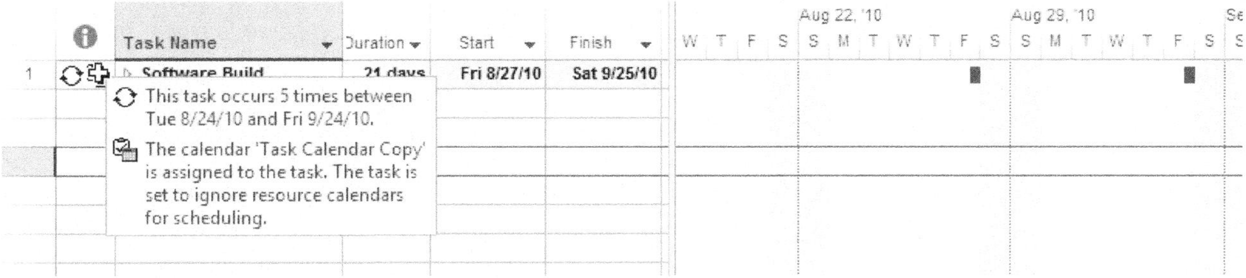


## Understanding Task Indicators

The different types of indicators.

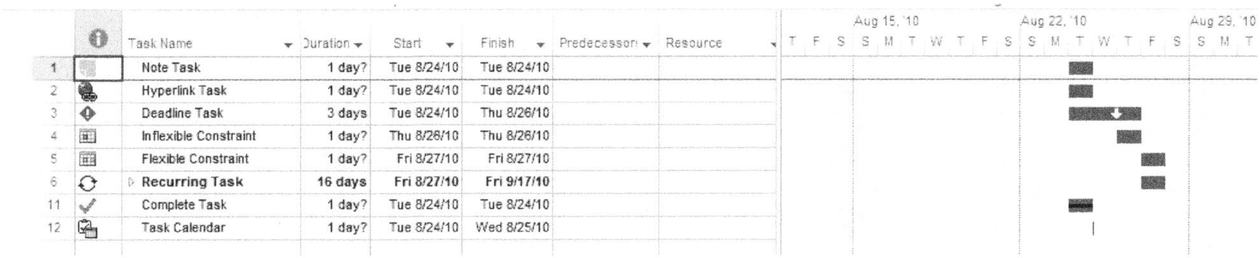

## Chapter 4 – Working with Resources

In this chapter, you will learn some advanced techniques for working with resources. You will need to be able to adjust some resource details to have Project develop an accurate schedule. For example, if one of your resources is not available for the first two weeks of a project, you will need to enter that information in Project to adjust the tasks for that resource accordingly. This chapter will also explain resource contours. You will also learn about resource calendars and availability dates, as well as how to group resources.

### Assigning a Resource Calendar

How to assign a new base calendar to the resource calendar.

Step 1: Change the view to the *Resource Sheet* by selecting **Resource Sheet** from the **View** tab.

Step 2: Double-click the resource for which you want to adjust the calendar to open the *Resource Information* dialog box.

Step 3: In the *Resource Information* dialog box, select **Change Working Time** button.

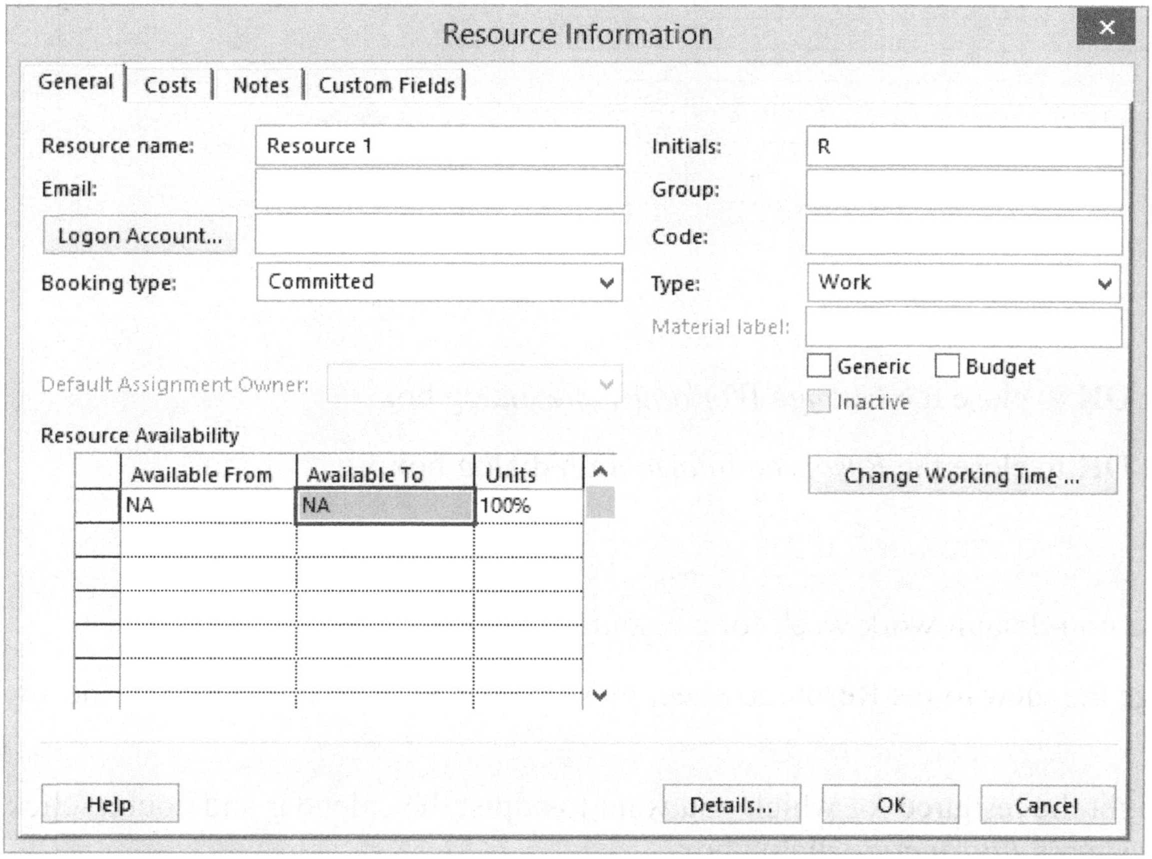

Step 4: Select a new **Base Calendar** from the drop down list.

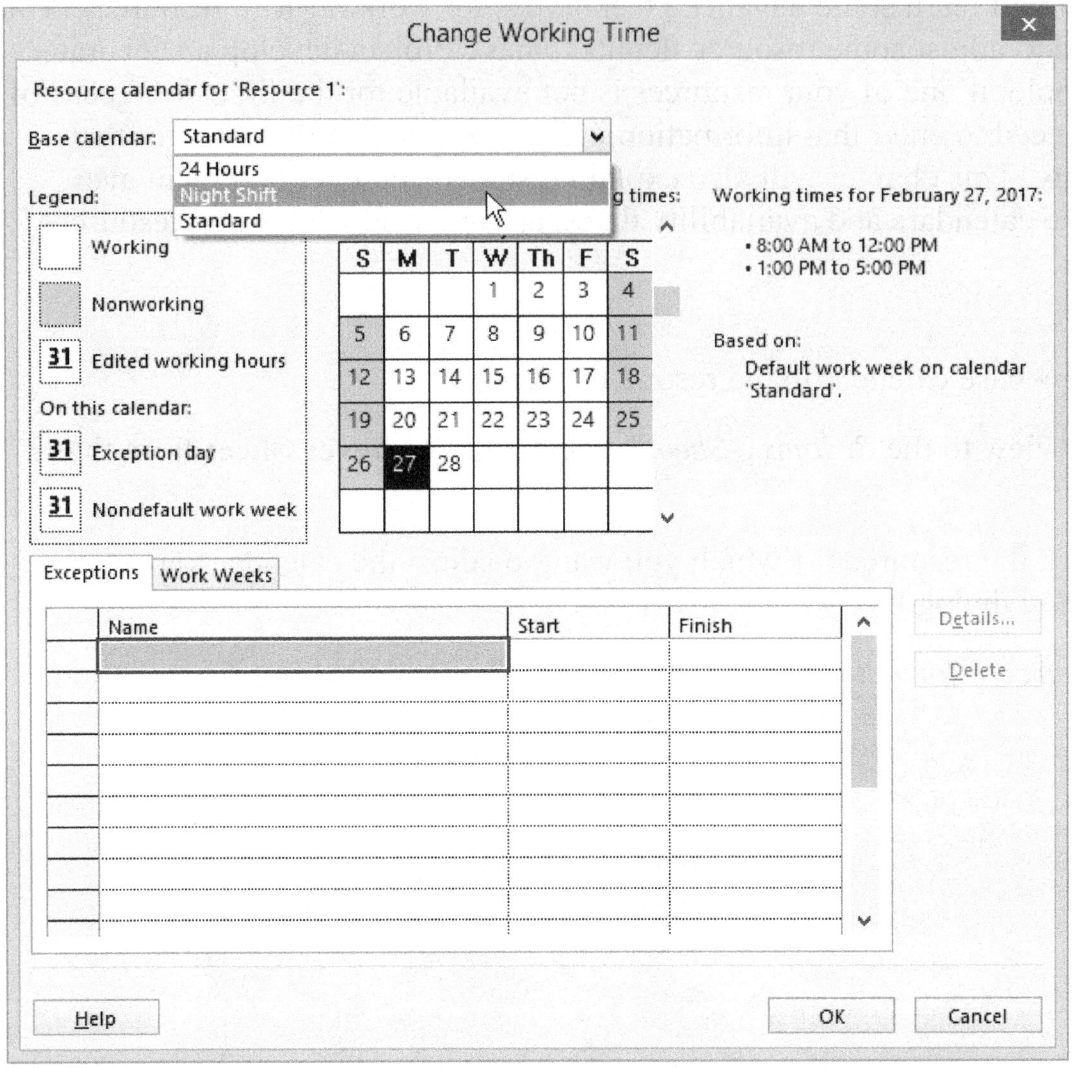


Step 5: Select **OK** to close the *Change Working Time* dialog box.

Step 6: Select **OK** to close the *Resource Information* dialog box.

## Customizing a Resource Calendar

How to enter a non-default work week for a resource calendar.

Step 1: Change the view to the Resource Sheet by selecting **Resource Sheet** from the **View** tab.

Step 2: Highlight the resource for which you want to adjust the calendar and double-click to open the *Resource Information* dialog box.

Step 3: In the *Resource Information* dialog box, select **Change Working Time** button.

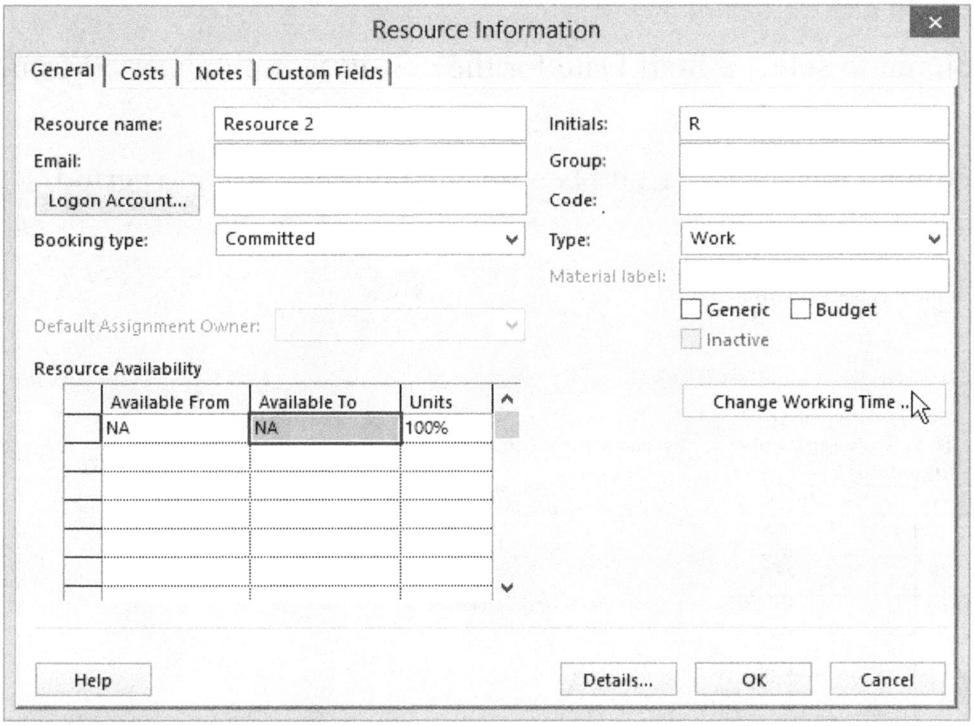


Step 4: Select the **Work Weeks** tab.

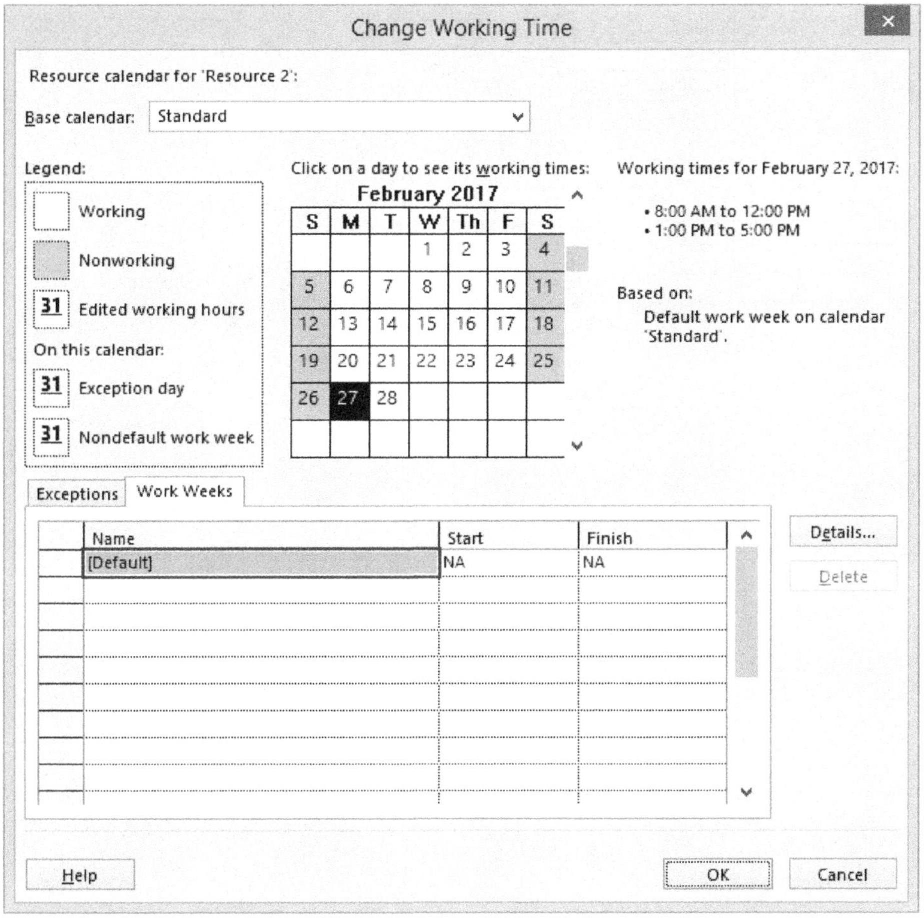

Step 5: Enter a **Name** for your reference to identify the work week. For example, you might call it "Finishing Project A."

Step 6: Select the **Start** column to select a Start Date for the non-default time period from the calendar.

Step 7: Select the **Finish** column to select an End Date for the non-default time period from the calendar.

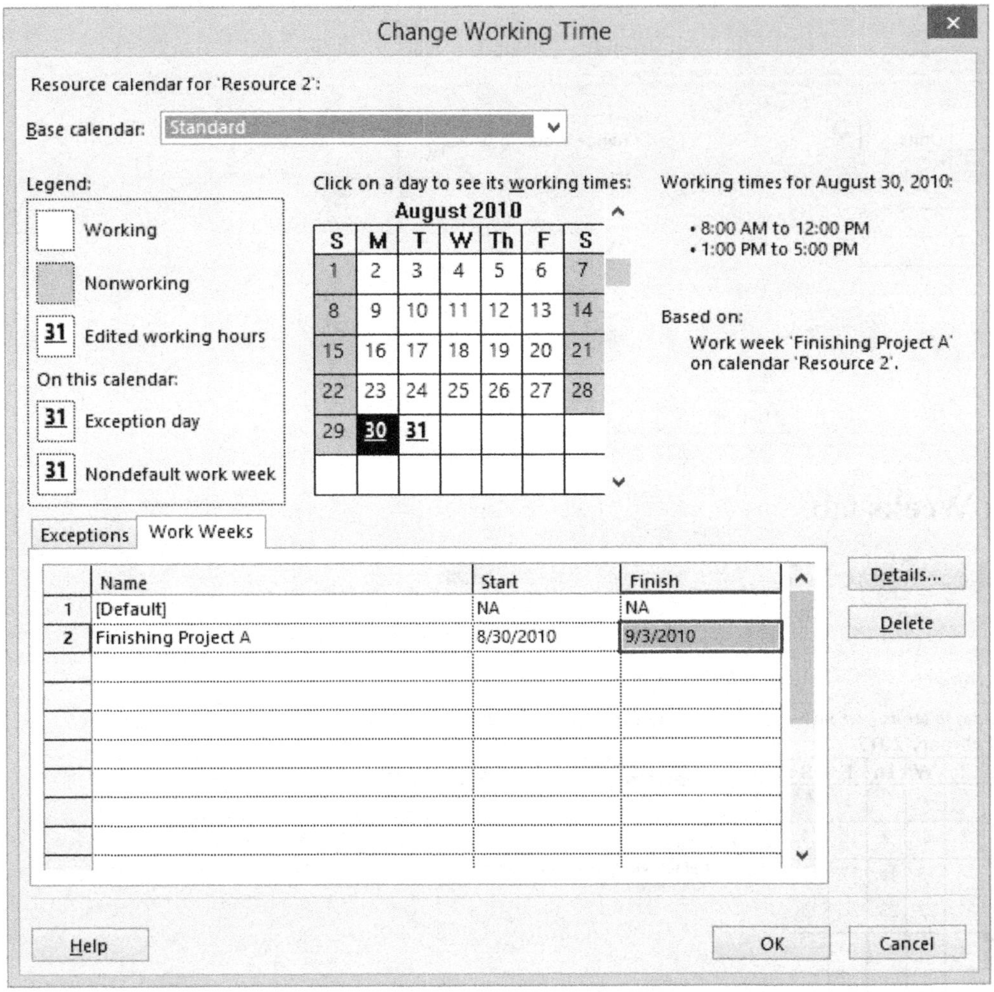

Step 8: Select **Details** to define the working hours for the selected work week.

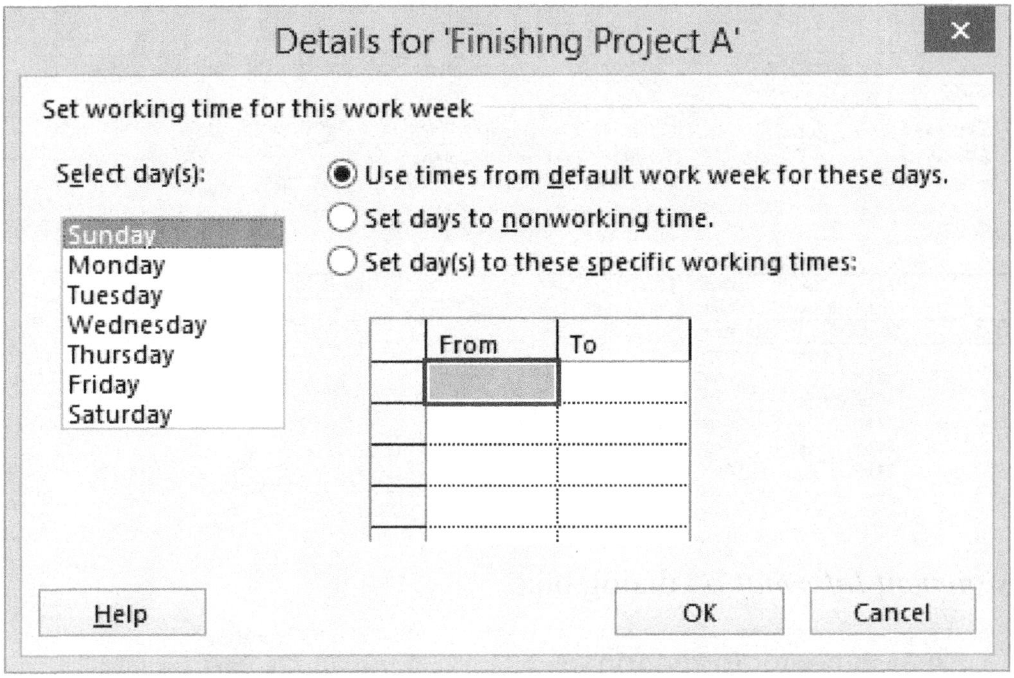


Step 9: Highlight the day or days (hold down the SHIFT or CTRL keys to select multiple days) that you want to define.

Step 10: Select either **Use times from default work week for these days, Set days to nonworking time**, or **Set day(s) to these specific working times**. If you select the third option, also enter the **Start** and **Finish** time for each working period on the selected day(s). Repeat this step to define each day of the week for the selected work week.

Step 11: Select **OK** to close the *Details* dialog box.

Step 12: Select **OK** to close the *Change Working Time* dialog box.

Step 13: Select **OK** to close the *Resource Information* dialog box.

## Applying Predefined Resource Contours

Use the following procedure to apply a contour.

Step 1: Select **Task Usage** from the **View** tab.

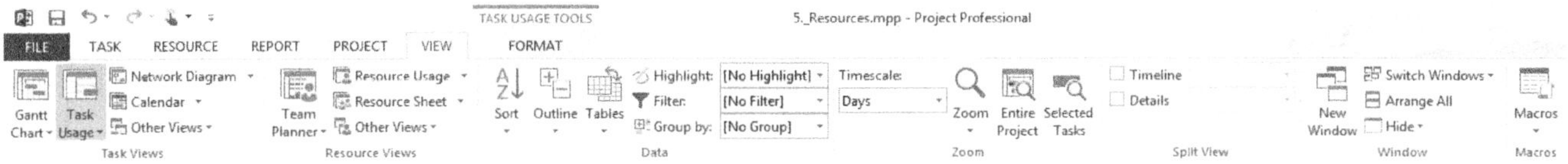

Step 2: Double-click on the resource assigned to the task that requires a contoured work assignment.

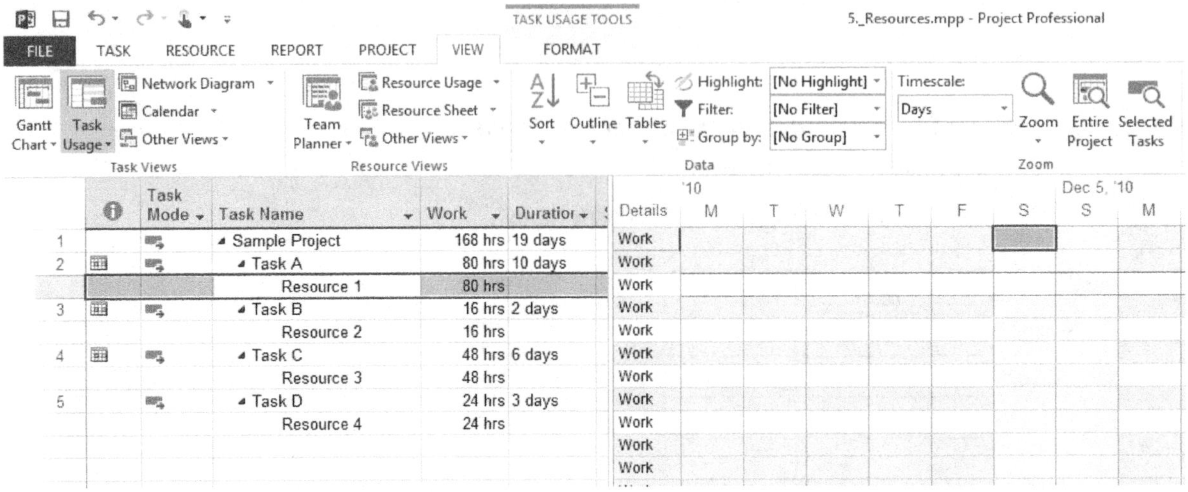


Project displays the *Assignment Information* dialog box.

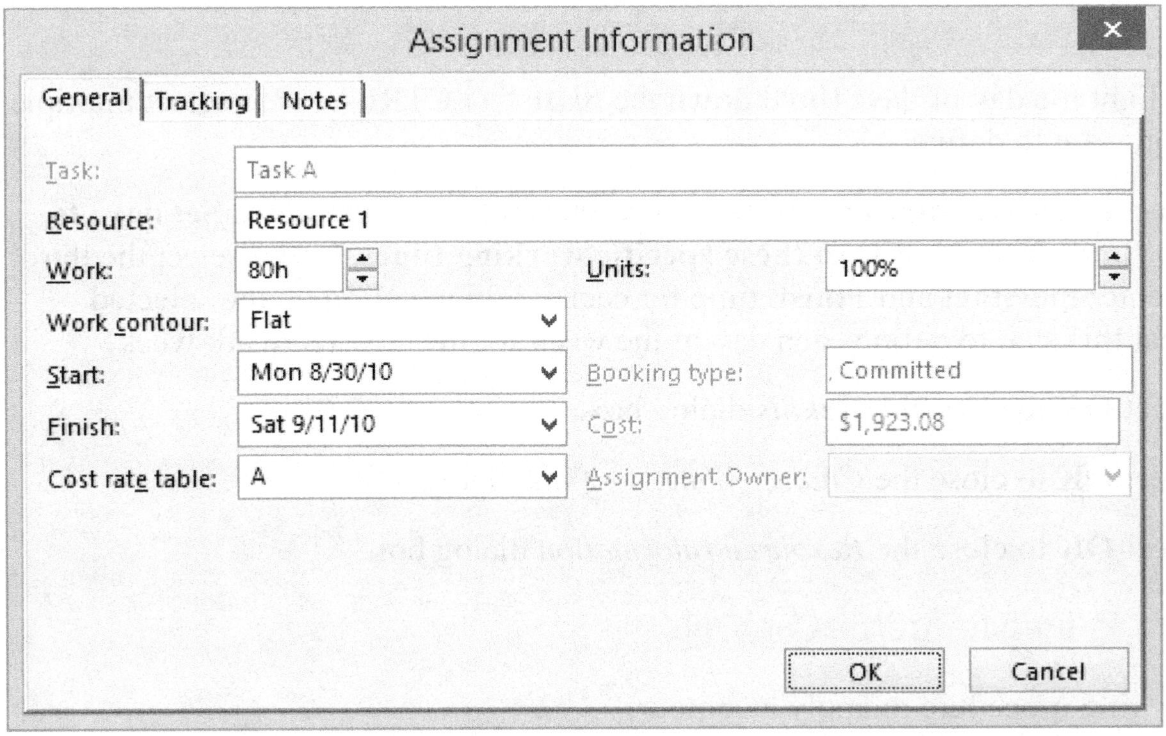


Step 3: In the **Work Contour** field, select an option from the drop down list.

Step 4: Select **OK**.

Project displays the contour indicator in the Indicator Column. It also redistributes the work for the selected task according to the selected contour.

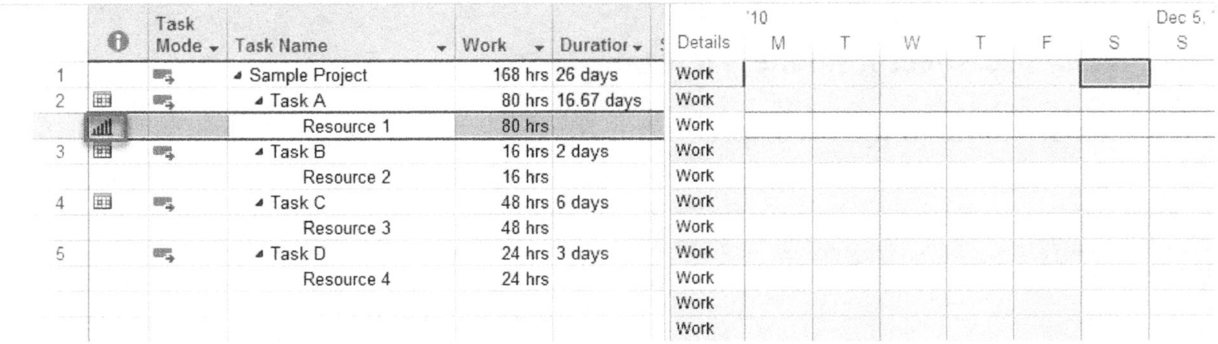


## Specifying Resource Availability Dates

How to indicate resource availability.

Step 1: Select **Resource Sheet** from the **View** tab.

Step 2: Double-click on the resource to open the *Resource Information* dialog box.

Step 3: Select the arrow under **Available From** to select a Start Date for the availability definition from the calendar.

Step 4: Select the arrow under **Available To** to select an End Date for the availability definition from the calendar.

Step 5: Select or enter the **Units** of availability as a percentage of full time.

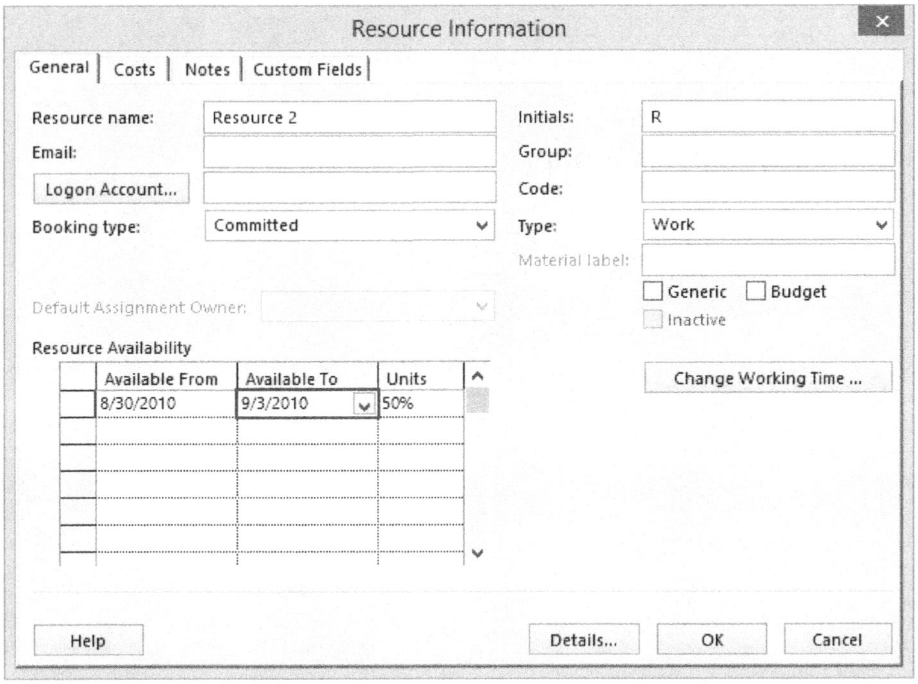


Step 6: Select **OK** to close the *Resource Information* dialog box.

## Grouping Resources

Use the following procedure to group resources.

Step 1: Select **Resource Sheet** from the **View** tab.

Step 2: Enter a group name in the **Group** column for each resource.

| | | Resource Name | Type | Material | Initials | Group | Max. | Std. Rate | Ovt. Rate | Cost/Use | Accrue | Base | Code | Add New Column |
|---|---|---|---|---|---|---|---|---|---|---|---|---|---|---|
| 1 | | Resource 1 | Work | | R | salary | 100% | $50,000.00/yr | $0.00/hr | $0.00 | Prorated | Night Shift | | |
| 2 | ◈ | Resource 2 | Work | | R | Salary | 0% | $50,000.00/yr | $0.00/hr | $0.00 | Prorated | Standard | | |
| 3 | | Resource 3 | Work | | R | hourly | 100% | $15.00/hr | $30.00/hr | $0.00 | Prorated | Standard | | |
| 4 | | Resource 4 | Work | | R | hourly | 100% | $15.00/hr | $30.00/hr | $0.00 | Prorated | Standard | | |

Step 3: Select the **Group By** drop down list.

Step 4: Select **Resource Group**.

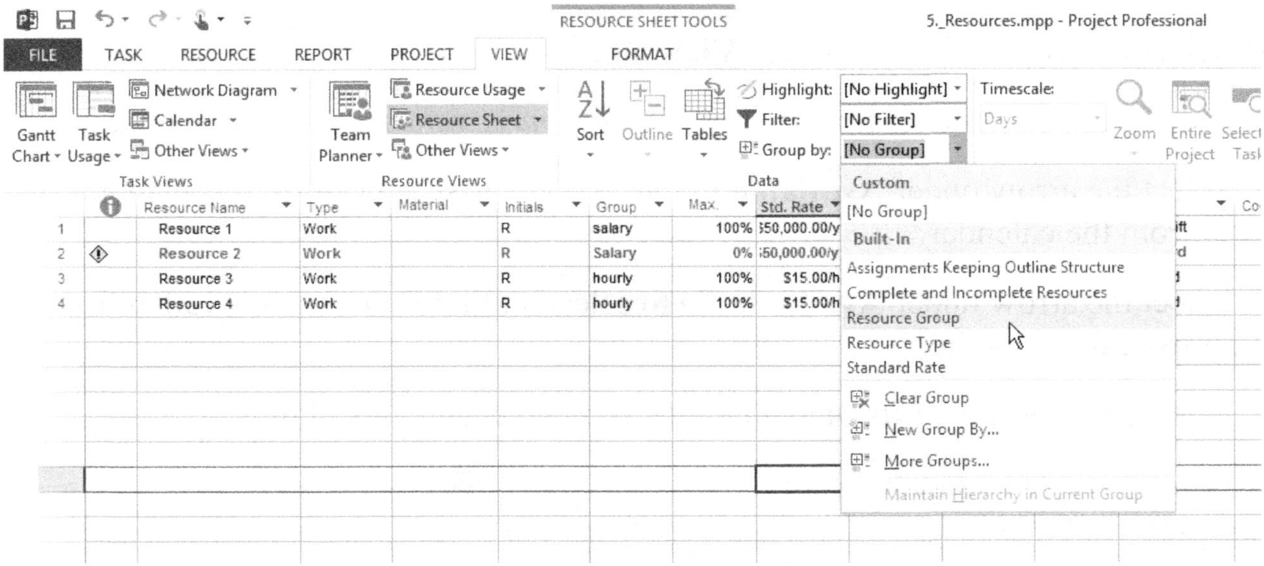


Project displays the resources in the appropriate group.

| | | Resource Name | Type | Material | Initials | Group | Max. | Std. Rate | Ovt. Rate | Cost/Use | Accrue | Base | Code | Add New Column |
|---|---|---|---|---|---|---|---|---|---|---|---|---|---|---|
| | | **Group: hourly** | | | | **hourly** | **200%** | | | **$0.00** | | | | |
| 3 | | Resource 3 | Work | | R | hourly | 100% | $15.00/hr | $30.00/hr | $0.00 | Prorated | Standard | | |
| 4 | | Resource 4 | Work | | R | hourly | 100% | $15.00/hr | $30.00/hr | $0.00 | Prorated | Standard | | |
| | | **Group: salary** | | | | **salary** | **100%** | | | **$0.00** | | | | |
| 1 | | Resource 1 | Work | | R | salary | 100% | $50,000.00/yr | $0.00/hr | $0.00 | Prorated | Night Shift | | |
| 2 | ◈ | Resource 2 | Work | | R | Salary | 0% | $50,000.00/yr | $0.00/hr | $0.00 | Prorated | Standard | | |

## Chapter 5 – Working with Costs

In order for Project to successfully calculate costs for a project, you must enter accurate information, including varying pay rates. A work resource has a standard pay rate and an overtime rate. You can also enter specific pay rates for a certain day or for an assignment. In this chapter, we will look at resource pay rates, including material resource consumption rates. Finally, we will look at entering task fixed costs.

### Adding Pay Rates for a Resource

Use the following procedure to enter pay rates.

Step 1: Select **Resource Sheet** from the **View** tab on the Ribbon.

Step 2: Enter the standard and overtime rate for each resource.

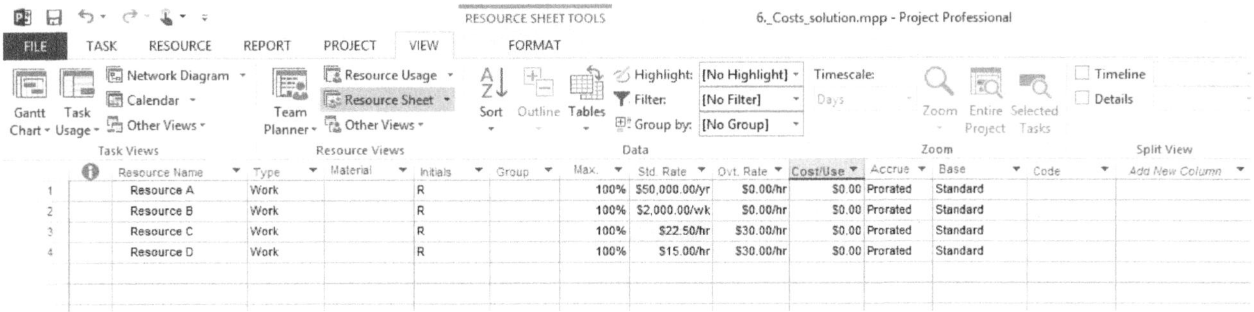


### Specifying Pay Rates for Different Dates

To enter a pay rate for a specific date, use the following procedure.

Step 1: Select **Resource Sheet** from the **View** tab on the Ribbon.

Step 2: Double-click the resource whose pay rate you want to define to open the *Resource Information* dialog box.

Step 3: Select the **Costs** tab.

Step 4: In the second row, enter the new standard, overtime, or a per use cost rate.

Step 5: Select the down arrow in the **Effective Date** column to select the effective date from the calendar.

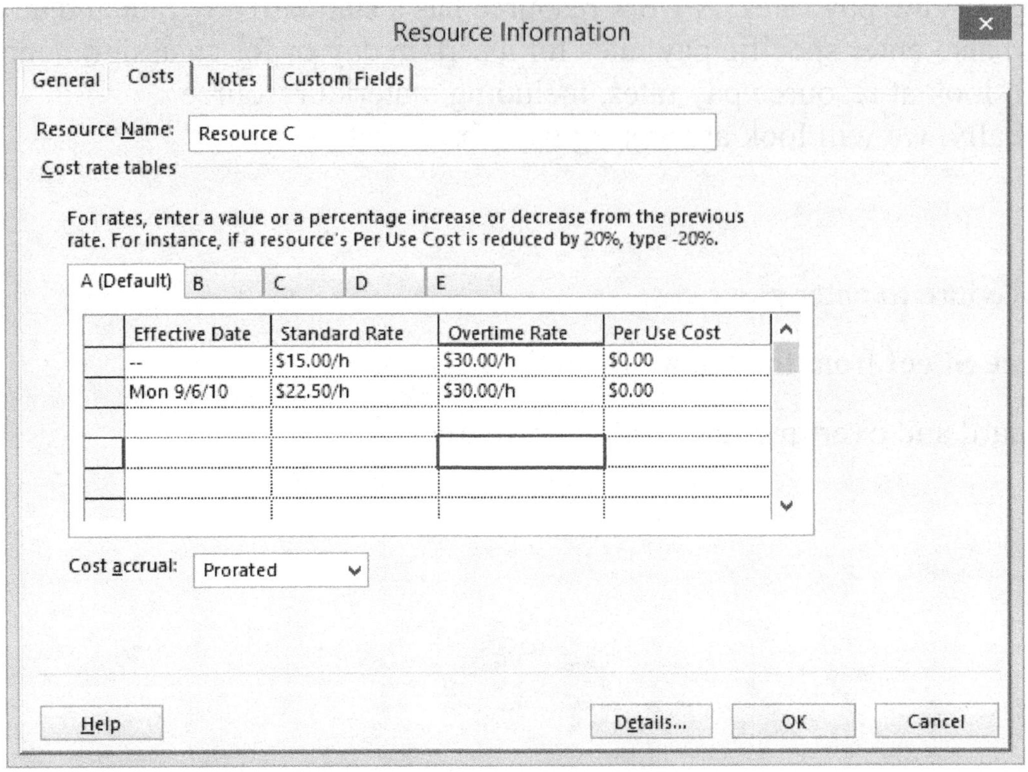


Step 6: Click on a lettered tab to enter additional cost rate tables. A is the default table. Repeat steps 4 and 5 for each table.

Step 7: Select **OK** to closet the *Resource Information* dialog box.

## Applying a Different Pay Rate to an Assignment

Use the following procedure to apply a different pay rate to an assignment

Step 1: Select **Task Usage** from the **View** tab to open the *Task Usage* sheet.

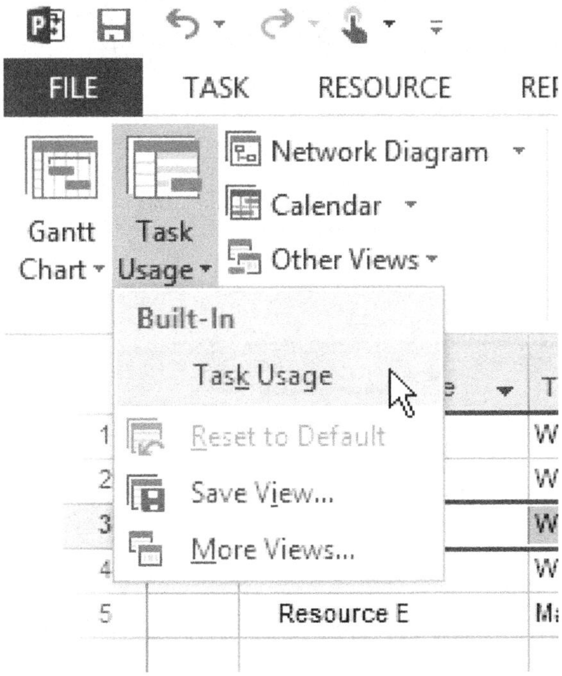


Step 2: Double-click on the resource assigned to the task that requires a different pay rate.

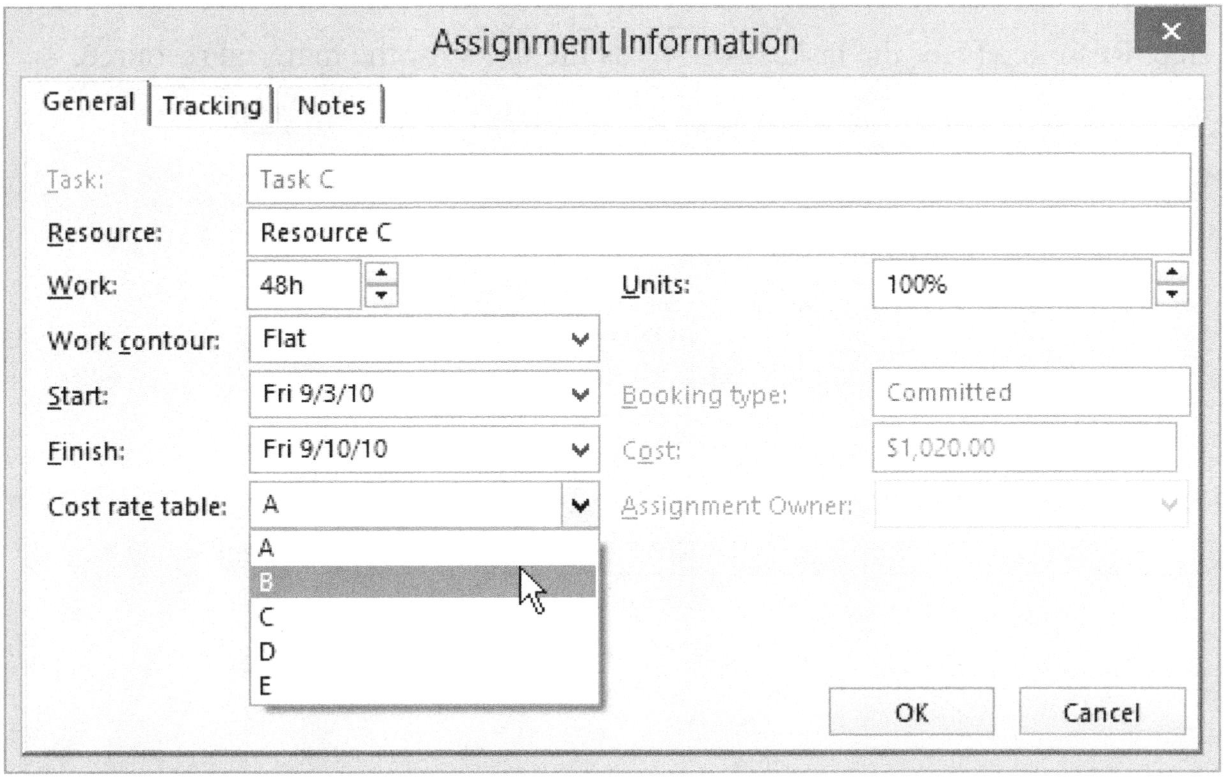

Project displays the *Assignment Information* dialog box.

Step 3: Select the **Cost Rate Table** that you want to use from the drop down list.

Step 4: Select **OK**.

If desired, return to the Gantt Chart view and show the participants the changed costs based on the new table. Project highlights the changes in the selected Changed Cell highlight color. (Note: the default highlight color is very light. You may want to change it using the Text Styles tool on the Format tab.)

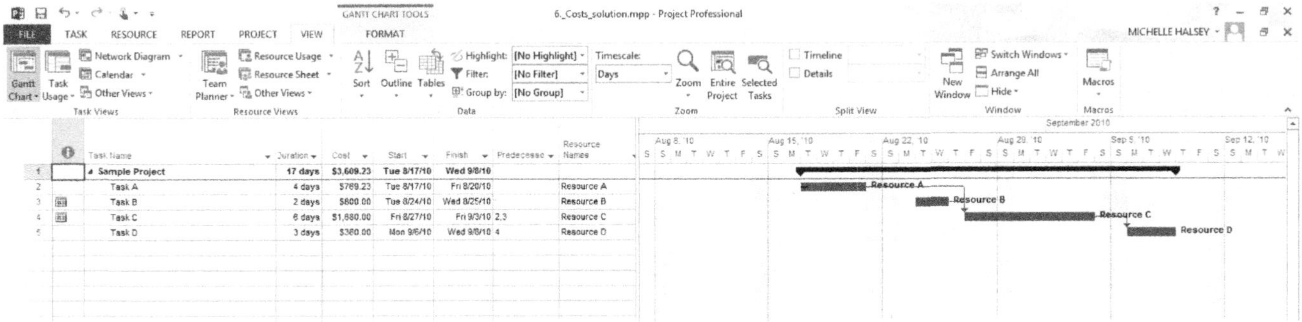


## Using Material Resource Consumption Rates

To assign a material resource to a task, use the following procedure.

Step 1: Double-click on the task to open the *Task Information* dialog box. In this example, select Task E.

Step 2: Select Resource E for the task. Enter 10 as the units for the material resource.

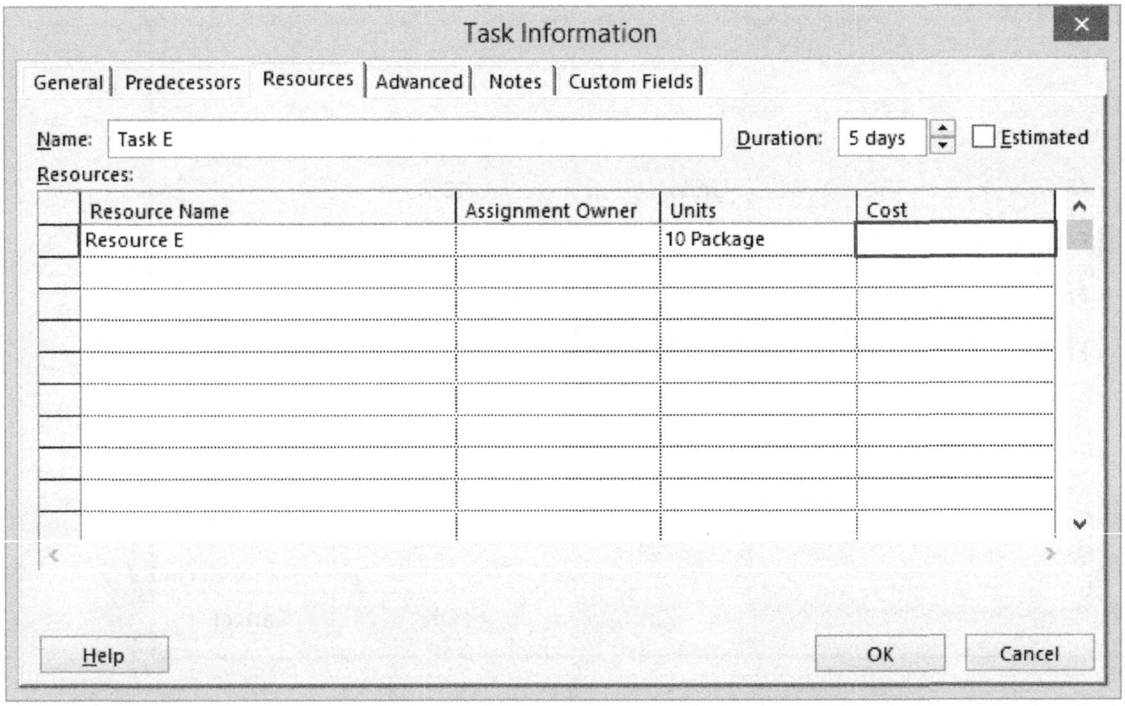

Step 3: Select **OK** to close the *Task Information* dialog box.

Step 4: Select **Task Usage** from the **View** tab.

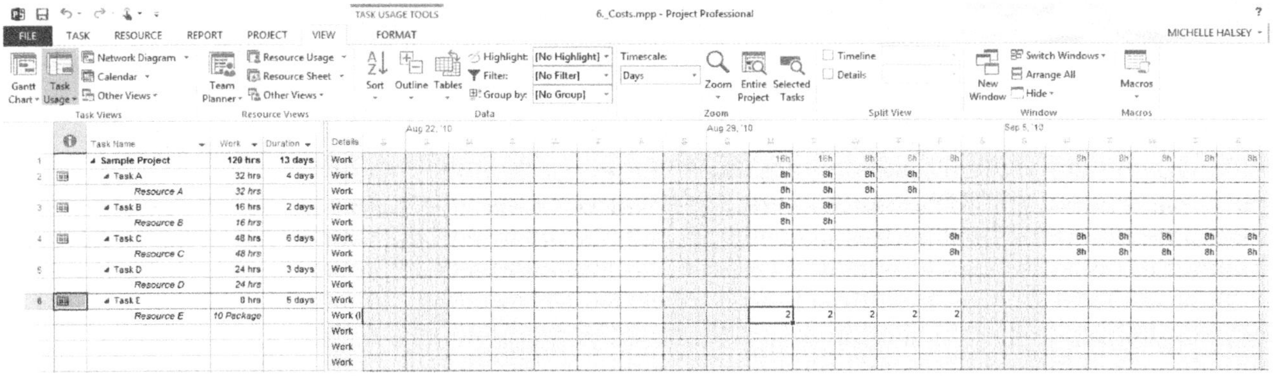


You can also manually override the calculated consumption rates by entering a new value in the columns for that resource for that task.

## Entering Task Fixed Costs

Use the following procedure to enter task fixed costs.

Step 1: Select **Table** from the View menu. Select **Cost**.

Step 2: Select the task for which you want to enter a fixed cost.

Step 3: Enter the amount in the **Fixed cost** column.

| | Task Name | Fixed | Fixed Cost | Total Cost | Baseline | Variance | Actual | Remaining |
|---|---|---|---|---|---|---|---|---|
| 1 | **Sample Project** | **$0.00** | **Prorated** | **$1,145.00** | **$0.00** | **$1,145.00** | **$0.00** | **$1,145.00** |
| 2 | Task A | $0.00 | Prorated | $0.00 | $0.00 | $0.00 | $0.00 | $0.00 |
| 3 | Task B | $0.00 | Prorated | $0.00 | $0.00 | $0.00 | $0.00 | $0.00 |
| 4 | Task C | $0.00 | Prorated | $1,020.00 | $0.00 | $1,020.00 | $0.00 | $1,020.00 |
| 5 | Task D | $25.00 | Prorated | $25.00 | $0.00 | $25.00 | $0.00 | $25.00 |
| 6 | Task E | $0.00 | Prorated | $100.00 | $0.00 | $100.00 | $0.00 | $100.00 |

# Chapter 6 – Balancing the Project

Project management involves constantly balancing opposing needs of costs, resources, and tasks to be done. In this chapter, we will look at some of the ways to balance a project, including both scheduling overtime for a resource and identifying and leveling resources that are over allocated. This chapter will explain how to level resources manually and automatically.

## Scheduling Resource Overtime

To enter overtime work, use the following steps.

Step 1: Select **Resource Usage** from the **View** tab of the Ribbon.

Step 2: Right-click the **Work** column and select **Insert Column** from the context menu.

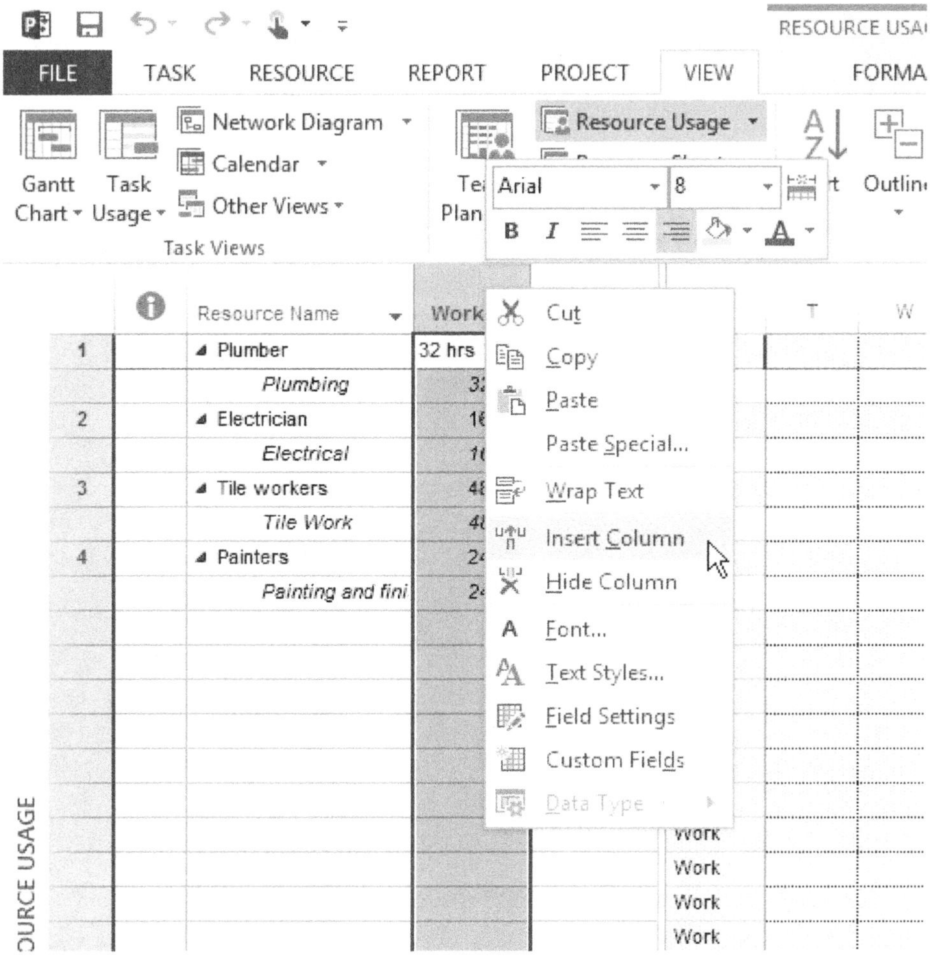

Step 3: Select **Overtime Work** from the **Field Name**-drop down list.

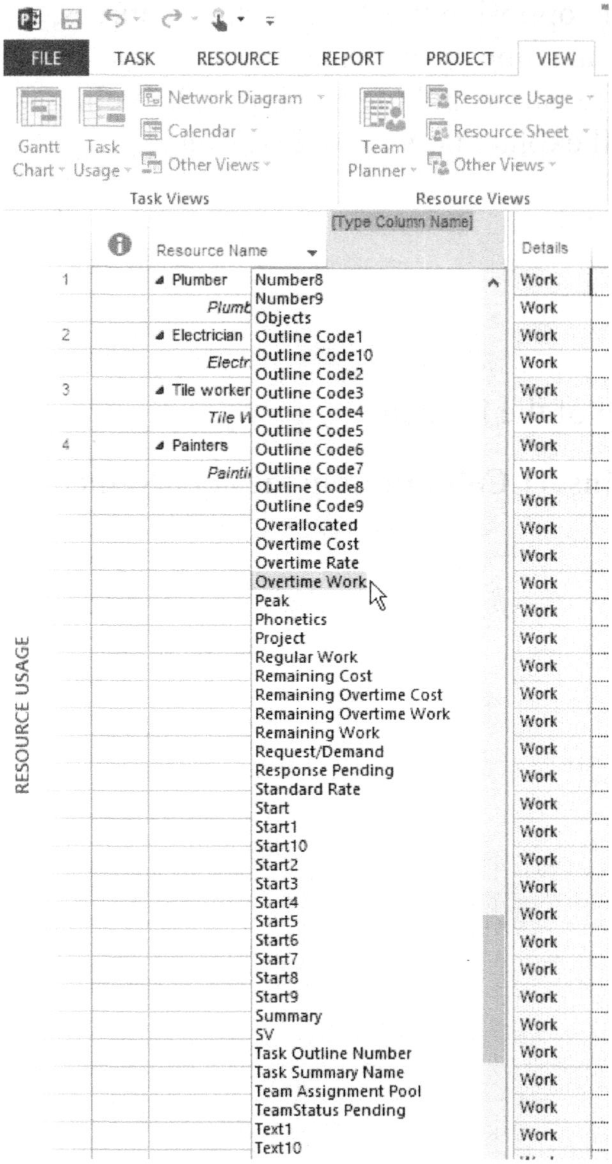

Step 4: In the **Overtime Work** column of the *Resource Usage* sheet, use the up and down arrows to adjust the number of overtime hours for each task.

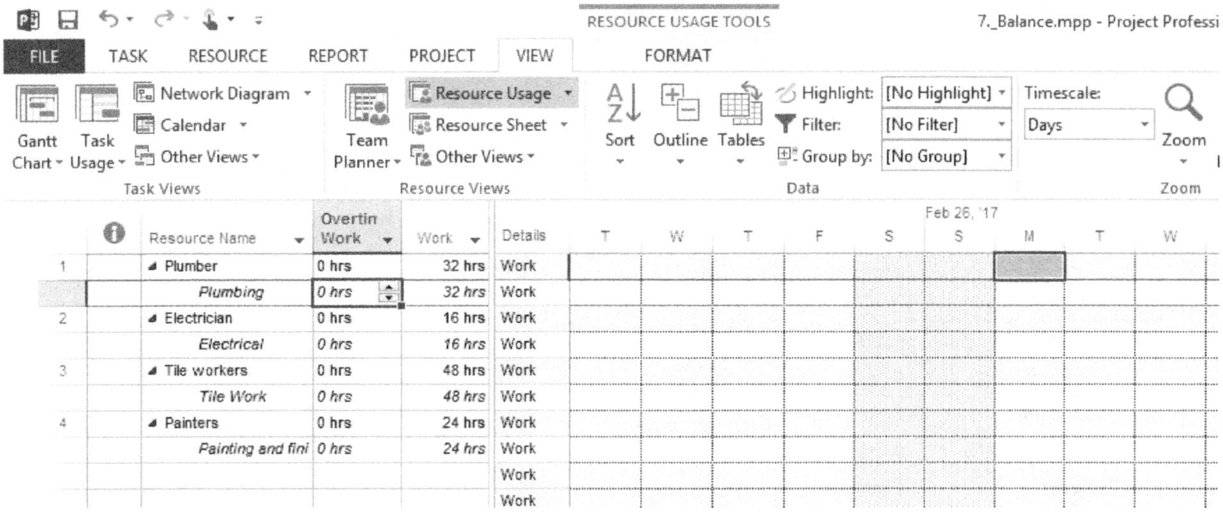


Project redistributes the work for the task to account for the overtime hours. The total duration for the task does not change.

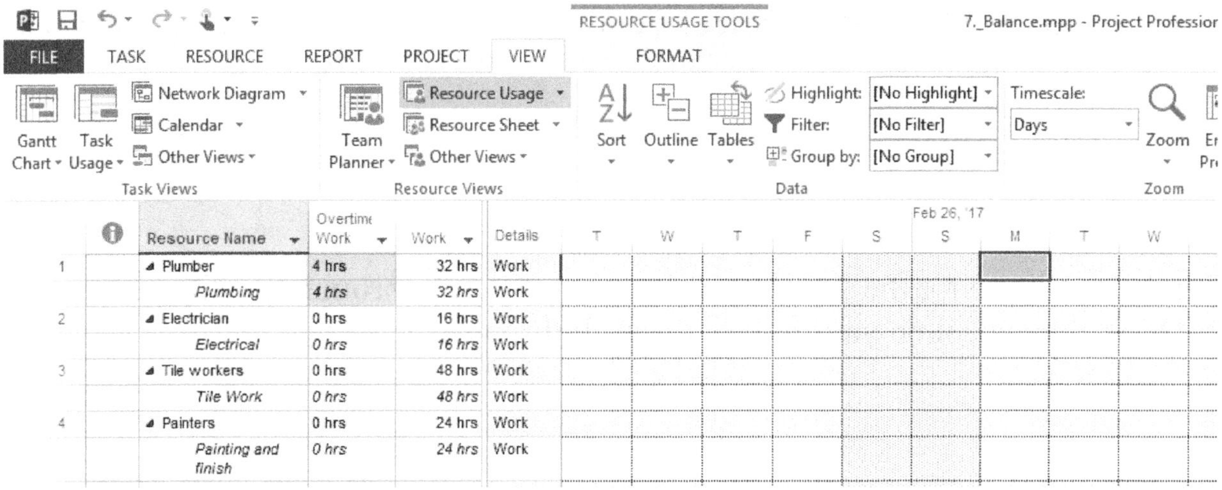


## Identifying Resource Over Allocation

Use the following procedure to review the resource graph.

Step 1: Select the **View** tab from the Ribbon.

Step 2: Select **Other Views** from the Resource area.

Step 3: Select **Resource Graph**.

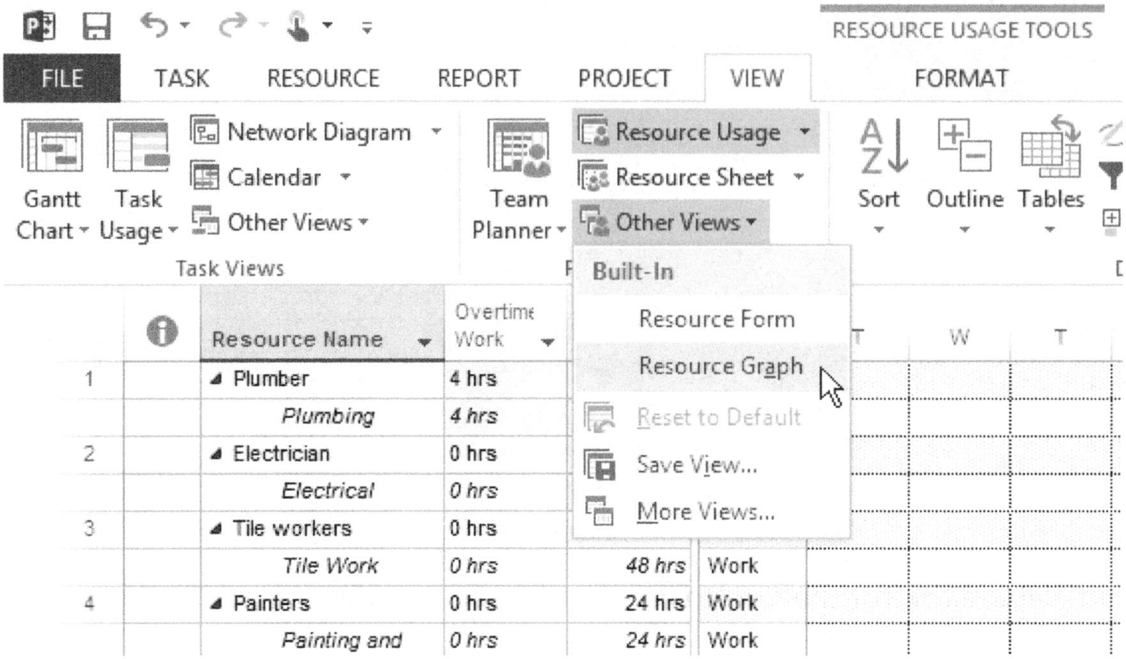


Step 4: Select the **Zoom Entire Project** tool from the **View** tab to show the right dates on the chart.

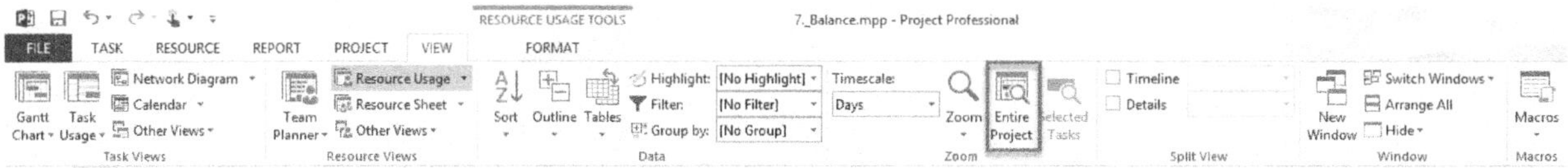


Step 5: Use the scroll bar for the left side of the chart to scroll through the different resources. Or use the wheel on your mouse to scroll through the resources.

The graph shows any resources that are over allocated as a percentage.

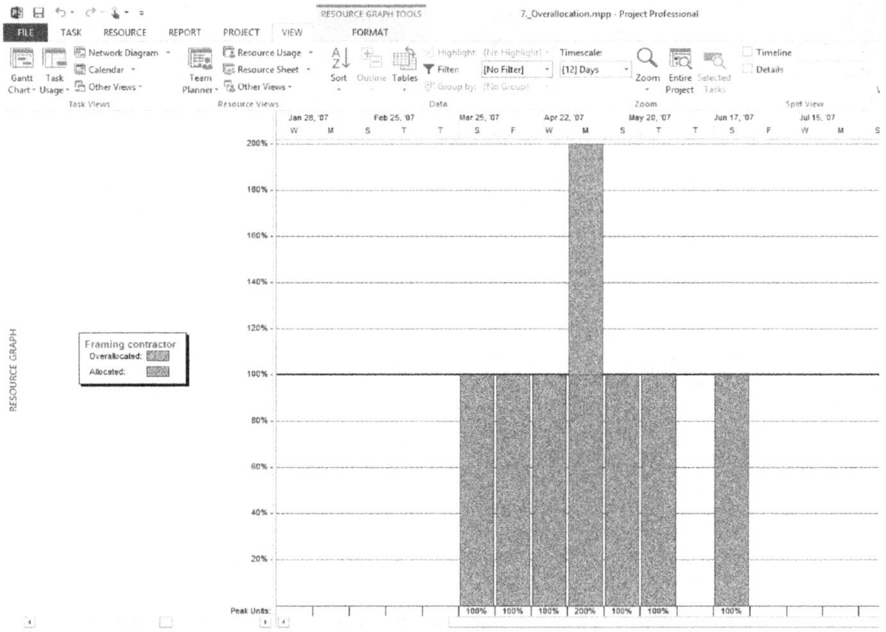


The Resource Sheet highlights over allocated resources in red.

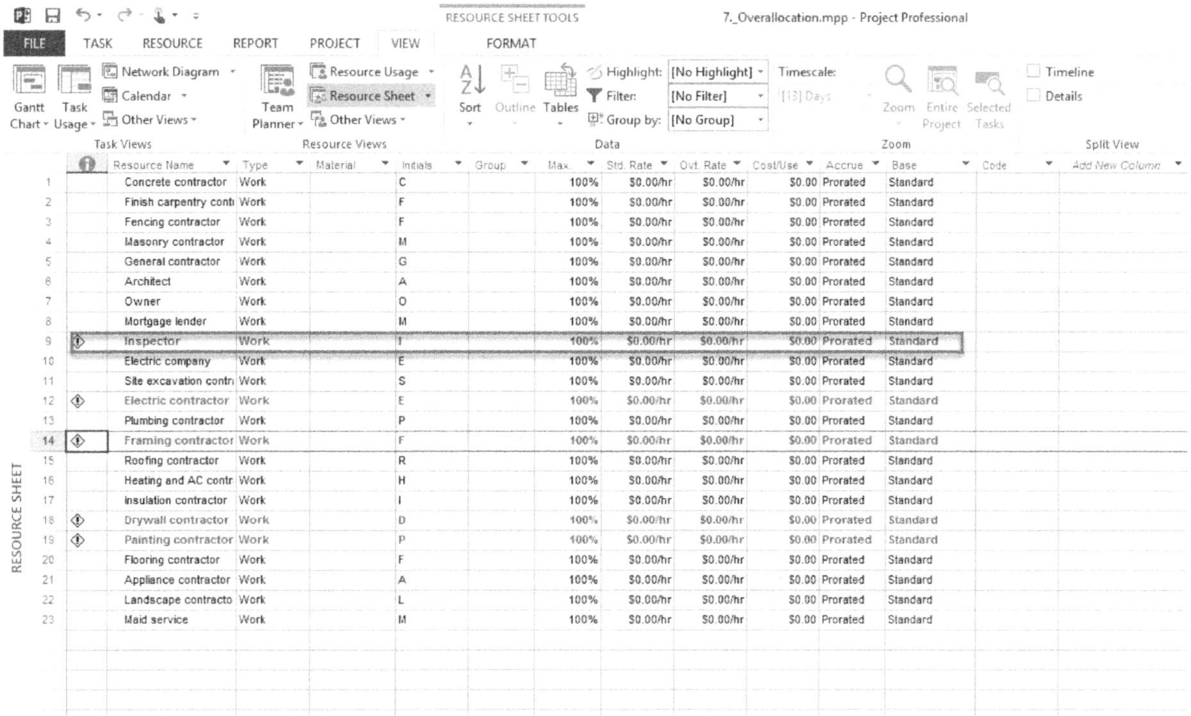


The Resource Usage sheet also highlights over allocated resources in red. You can expand the tasks for each resource to see which overlapping tasks result in an over allocation.

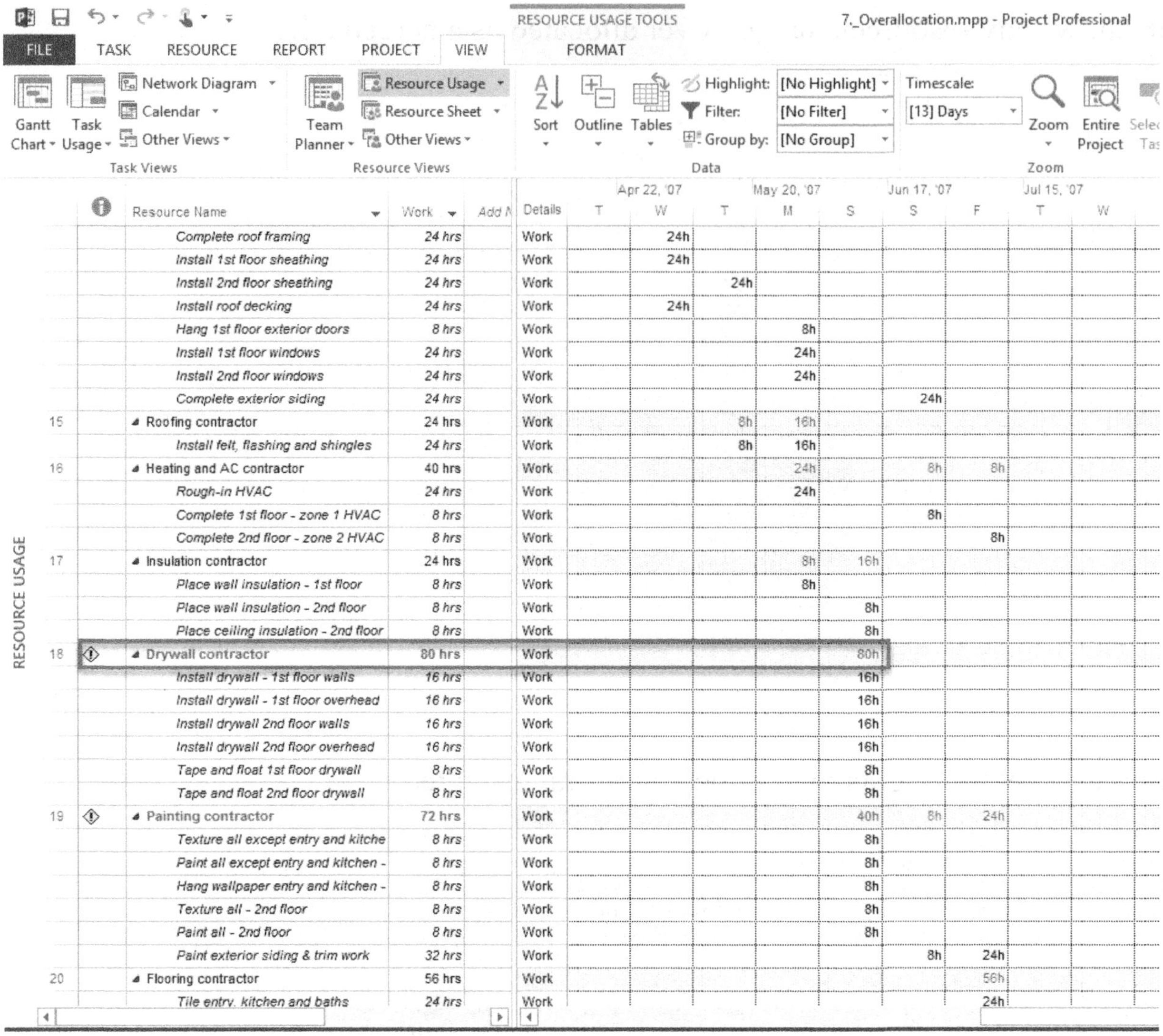

## Setting Leveling Options

Use the following procedure to open the *Resource Leveling* dialog box.

Select **Resource Usage** from the **View** tab. You can start from another view, but this view allows you to see the number of hours for each task. It also highlights the over allocated resources in red.

Step 1: Select the **Resource** tab from the Ribbon.

Step 2: Select **Leveling Options**.

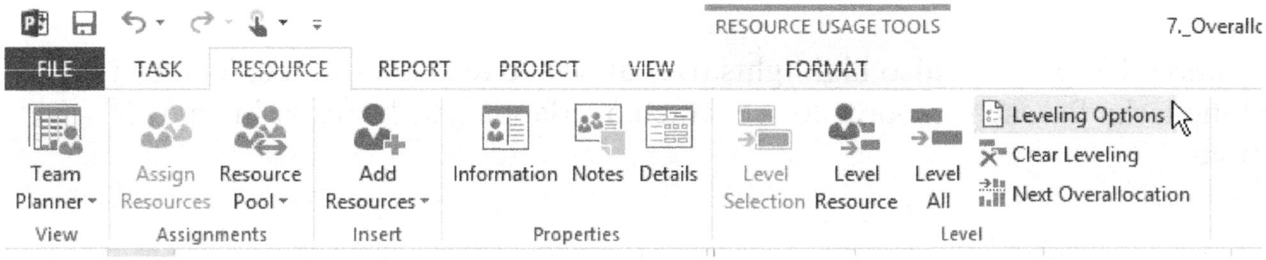

Project displays the *Resource Leveling* dialog box.

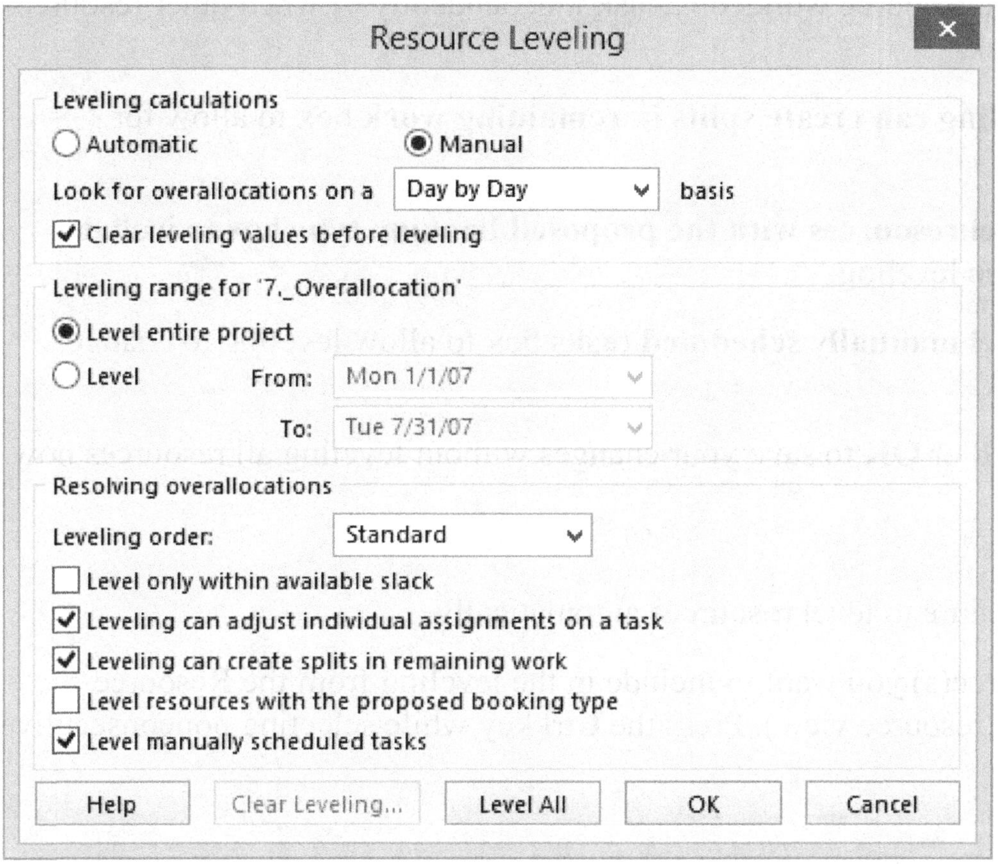


Step 3: Choose either **Automatic** or **Manual**. If you choose Automatic, make sure to clear the **Clear leveling values before leveling** checkbox. This way, Project will not clear previous leveling changes before making new changes to future over allocated resources.

Step 4: Select an option to indicate how you want Project to **Look for Over allocations** from the drop down list. **Day by Day** is the default selection. For this example, choose **Hour by Hour**.

Step 5: Select whether to level the entire project or a selected date range. If you choose the second option, select the **From** and **To** dates from the drop down calendars.

Step 6: Select a **Leveling order** from the drop down list. The Standard method examines predecessor dependencies, slack, dates, priorities, and constraints. **ID Only** looks at tasks in ascending order of ID number to look for places to level. **Priority**, **Standard** looks at priority level of the tasks first before considering the other criteria.

Step 7: Check the **Level only within available slack** box to prevent a delay of your project finish date. If this box is checked, you may get an error message if Project cannot find enough slack time to level the schedule.

Step 8: Check the **Leveling can adjust individual assignments on a task** box to allow leveling to adjust when a resource works on a task independently of when other resources working on the same task.

Step 9: Check the **Leveling can create splits in remaining work** box to allow for interruptions in tasks.

Step 10: Check the **Level resources with the proposed booking type** box to include proposed resources in the leveling.

Step 11: Check the **Level manually scheduled tasks** box to allow leveling to change manually scheduled tasks.

Step 12: Select **Level All** or **OK** to save your changes without leveling all resources now.

## Balancing Resource Over Allocations Automatically

Use the following procedure to level resources automatically.

Step 1: Select the resource(s) you want to include in the leveling from the Resource Usage sheet (or another resource view). Press the Ctrl key while selecting nonconsecutive resources.

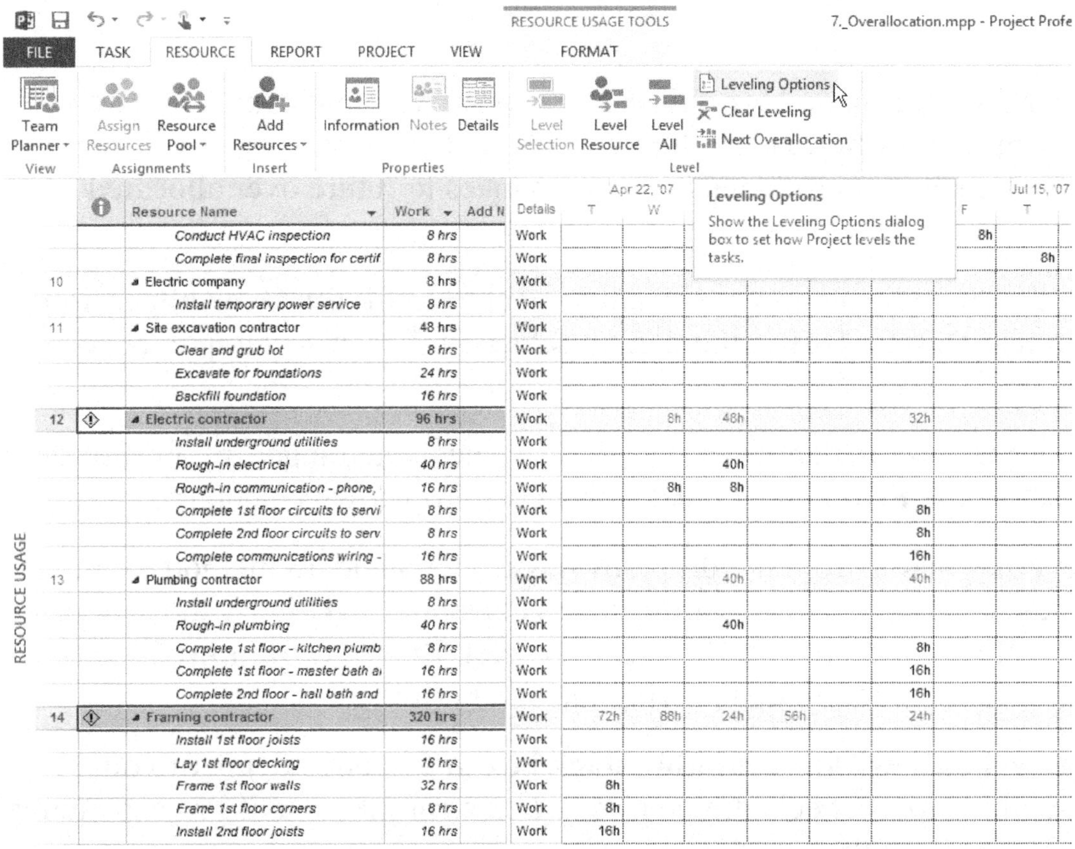


Step 2: Open the *Resource Leveling* dialog box (from the previous topic).

Step 3: Select **Automatic**.

Step 4: Set the other leveling options (see the previous topic for more information).

Step 5: Select **Level All**.

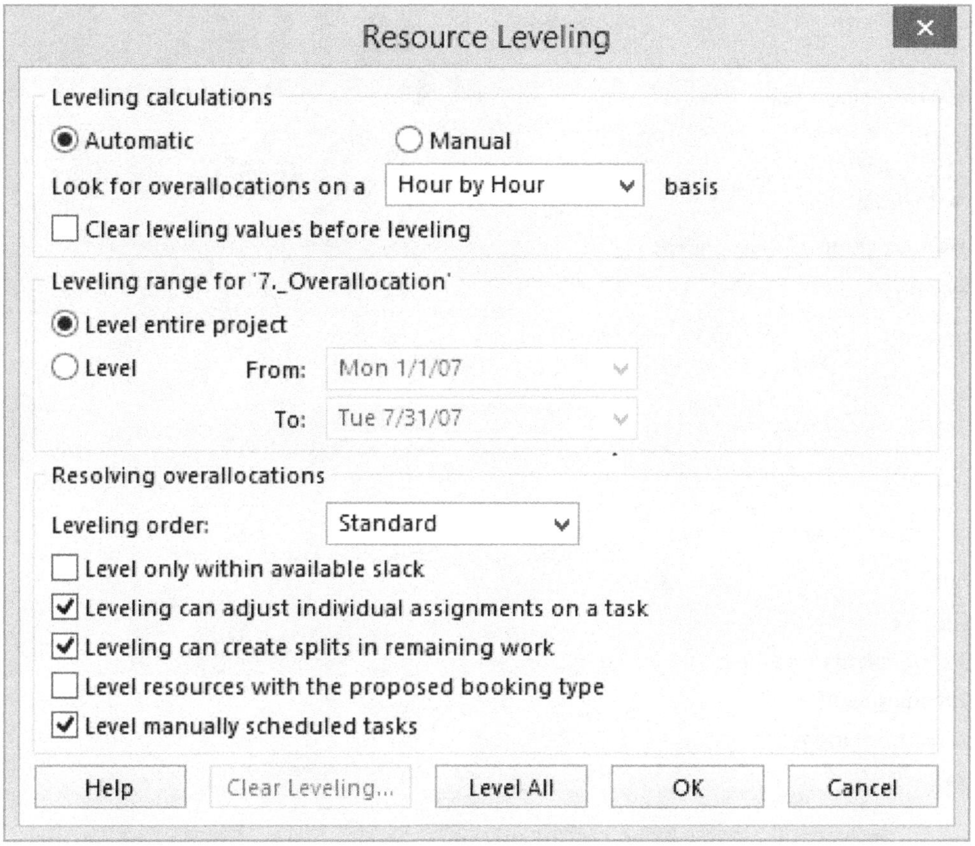


Project levels the selected resources now, but it will also level any future changes or additions that cause the selected resource(s) to be over allocated.

## Balancing Resource Over Allocations Manually

Use the following procedure to clear previous leveling.

Step 1: Select the **Resource** tab from the Ribbon.

Step 2: Select **Clear Leveling**.

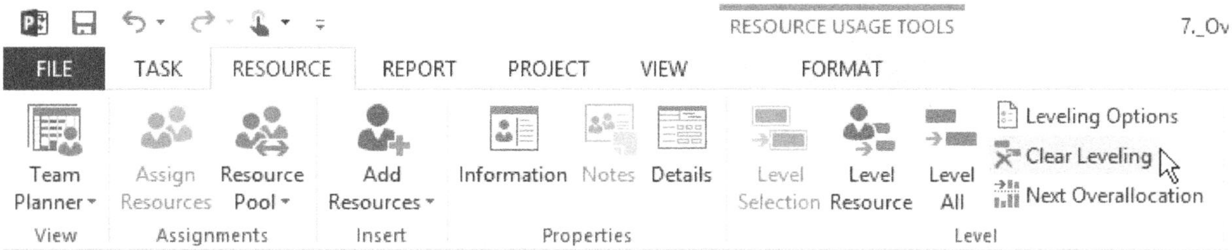


To level resources manually one resource at a time.

Step 1. Open the *Resource Leveling* dialog box (from the previous topic).

Step 2: Select **Manual**.

Step 3: Set the other leveling options (see the previous topics for more information).

Step 4: Select **OK**.

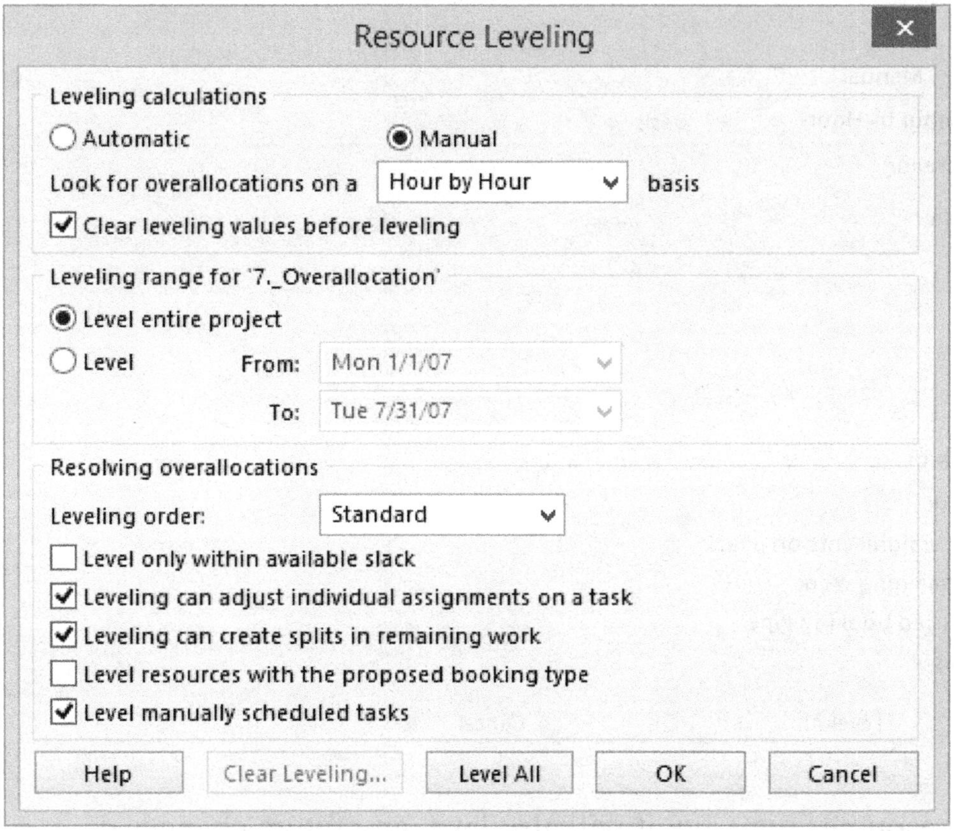


Step 5: Select the resource you want to level.

Step 6: Select **Level Resource** from the **Resource** tab on the Ribbon.

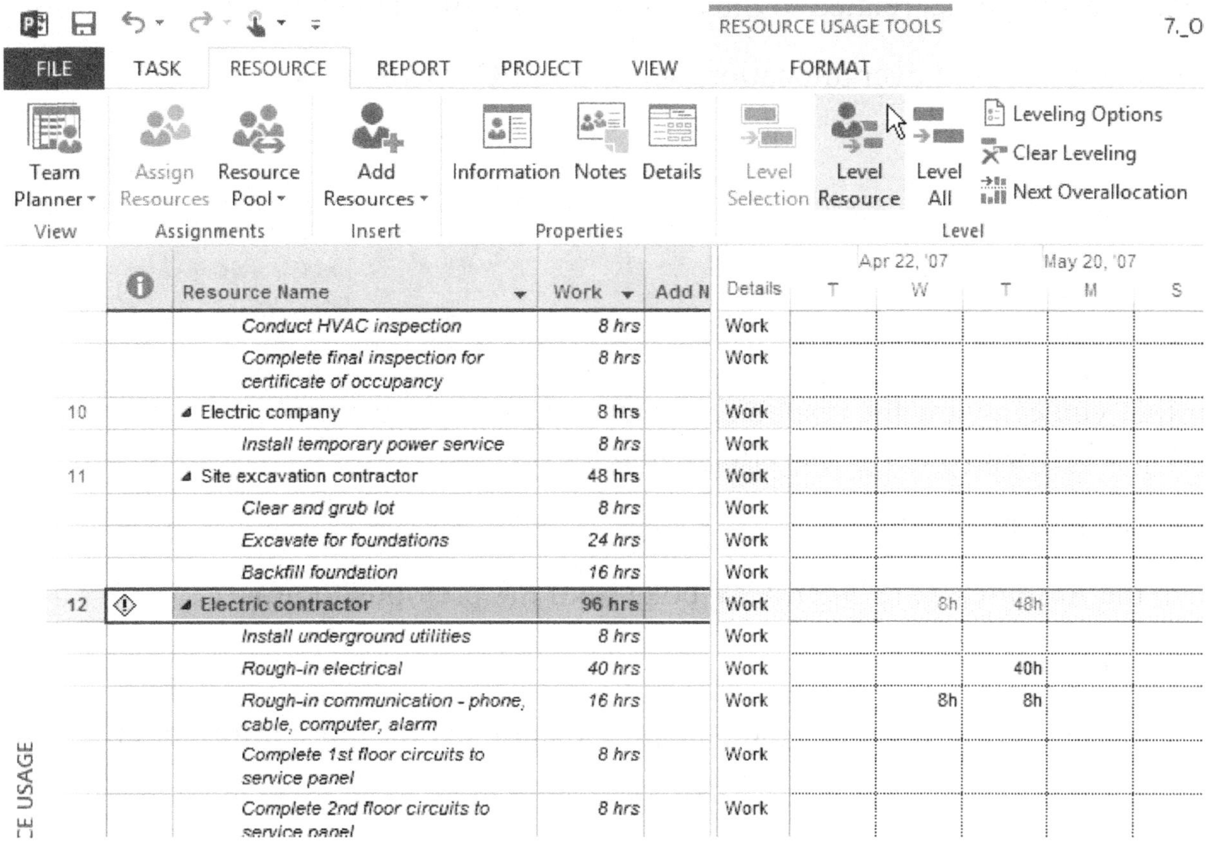


Step 7: Project displays the Level Resource dialog box.

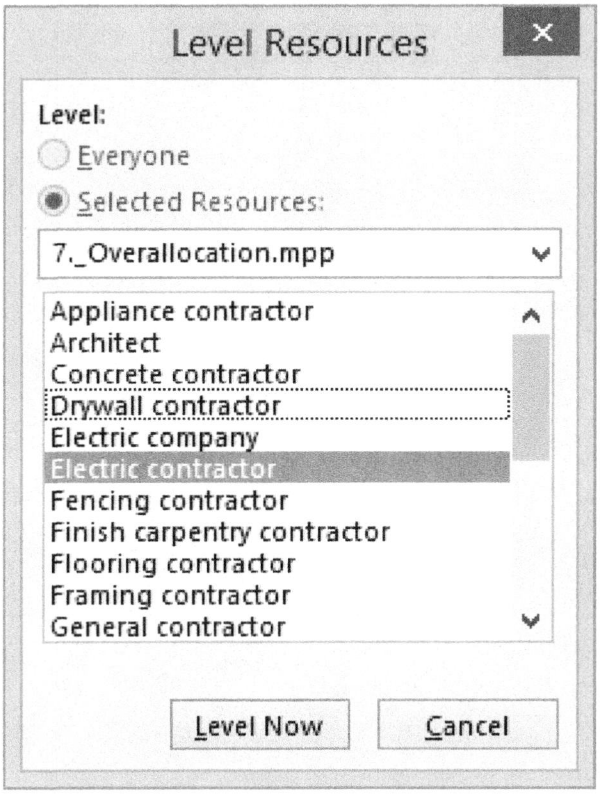

Step 8: Make sure the resource you want to level is highlighted and select **Level Now**. Project reschedules the tasks related to the over allocation of that resource.

Step 9: To move to the next over allocation, select **Next Overallocation**.

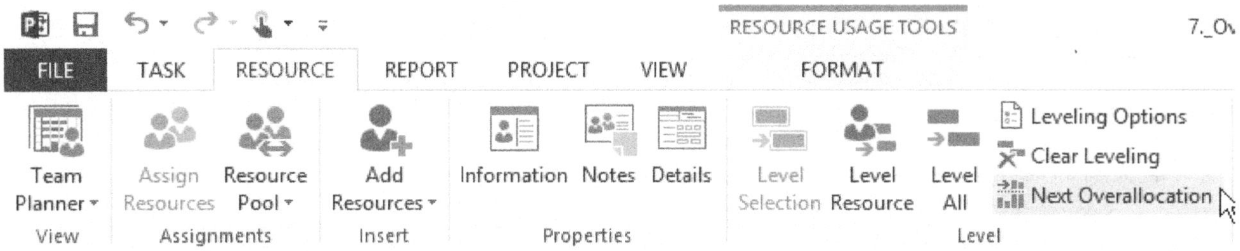


Remember that you can view the results of the leveling both by reviewing the Resource Usage sheet and by reviewing the Leveling Gantt view.

To level all resources manually.

Step 1: Open the *Resource Leveling* dialog box (from the previous topic).

Step 2: Select **Manual**.

Step 3: Set the other leveling options (see the previous topics for more information).

Step 4: Select **OK**.

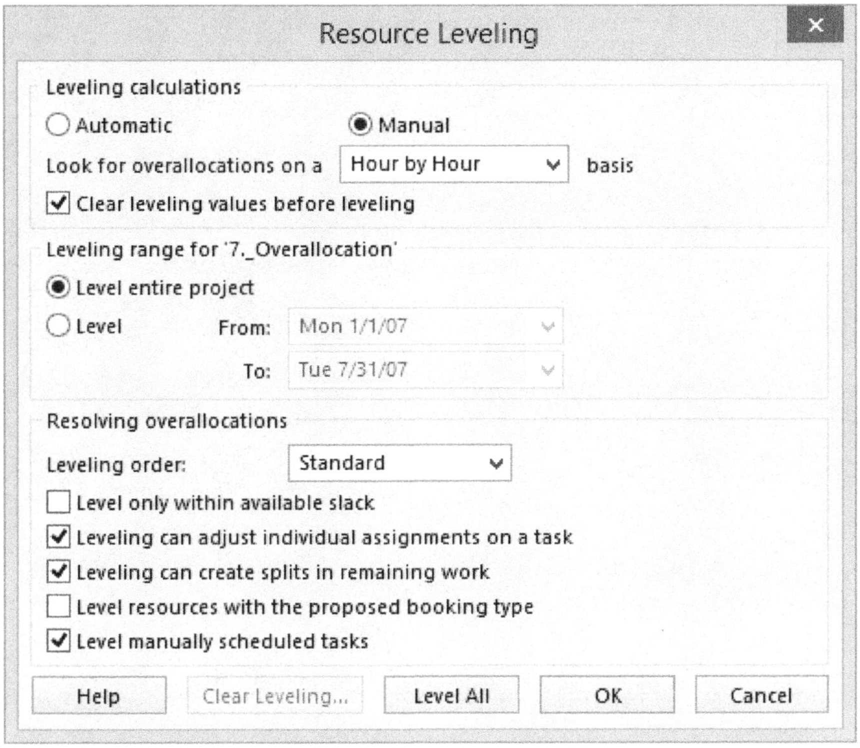


Step 5: Select **Level All** from the **Resource** tab on the Ribbon.

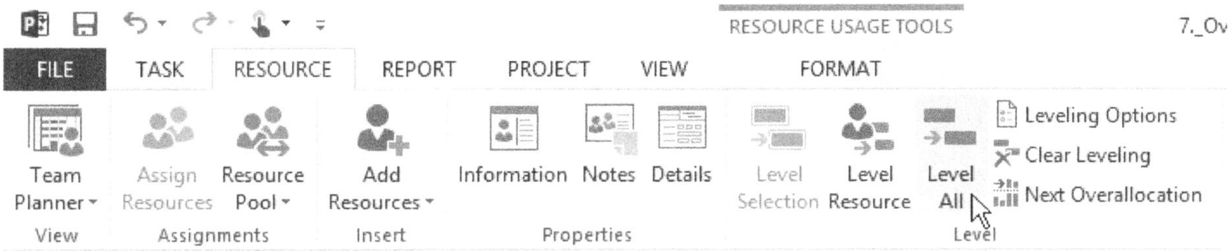


Project reschedules the tasks related to the over allocation of all resources.

Remember that you can view the results of the leveling both by reviewing the Resource Usage sheet and by reviewing the Leveling Gantt view.

# Chapter 7 – Updating Project Progress

This chapter covers updating the project progress. You will learn how to save a baseline plan to use as comparison as you review the progress of your project. This chapter also explains how to update the entire project. You will also learn how to update the specifics of a project, including task actual values, completion percentages, actual work, and actual costs.

## Saving a Baseline Plan

Use the following procedure to set a baseline.

Step 1: Enter the tasks, durations, and other details of your base project before setting a baseline.

Step 2: To set a baseline for selected tasks, select the tasks you want to track from the Gantt chart view.

Step 3: Select the Project tab from the Ribbon.

Step 4: Select **Set Baseline**. Select the **Set Baseline** option.

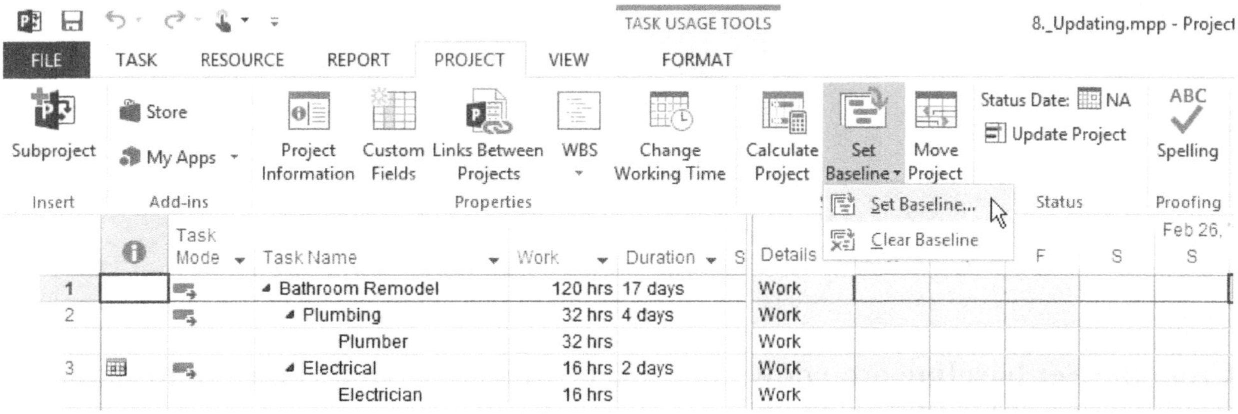

Project displays the *Set Baseline* dialog box.

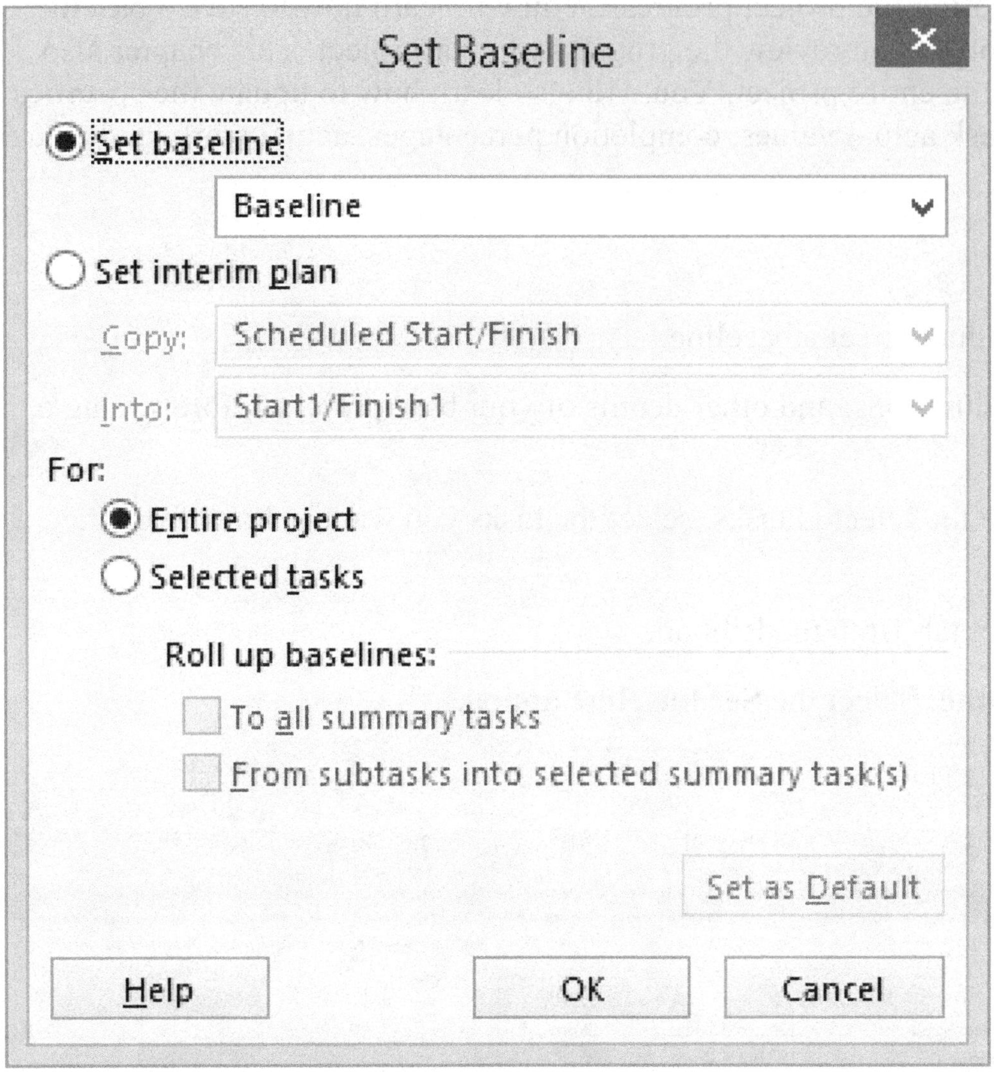


Step 5: From the **Set baseline** drop down list, select which baseline you want to set. You have the choice of the default baseline, or up to 10 other baselines, which are numbered 1 – 10.

Step 6: Select **Entire Project** or **Selected tasks**.

Step 7: If you select **Selected Tasks**, indicate how to roll up the baselines by checking the **To all summary tasks** box and/or the **From subtasks into selected summary task(s)** box.

Step 8: Select **OK**.

The Baseline column stores the baseline information. To add the Baseline column to see the baseline information. Use the following procedure.

Step 1: Right-click a column in the Gantt Chart view and select **Insert Column** from the context menu.

Step 2: Select a field to enter from the **Field name** drop down list. For each baseline you can set, you can enter the following columns to your table:

- Baseline Budget Costs
- Baseline Budget Work
- Baseline Cost
- Baseline Duration
- Baseline Finish
- Baseline Fixed Cost
- Baseline Fixed Cost Accrual
- Baseline Start
- Baseline Work

Step 3: Select **OK**. Repeat to add more baseline information to your current view.

The selected baseline column(s) display the baseline values for the selected task(s).

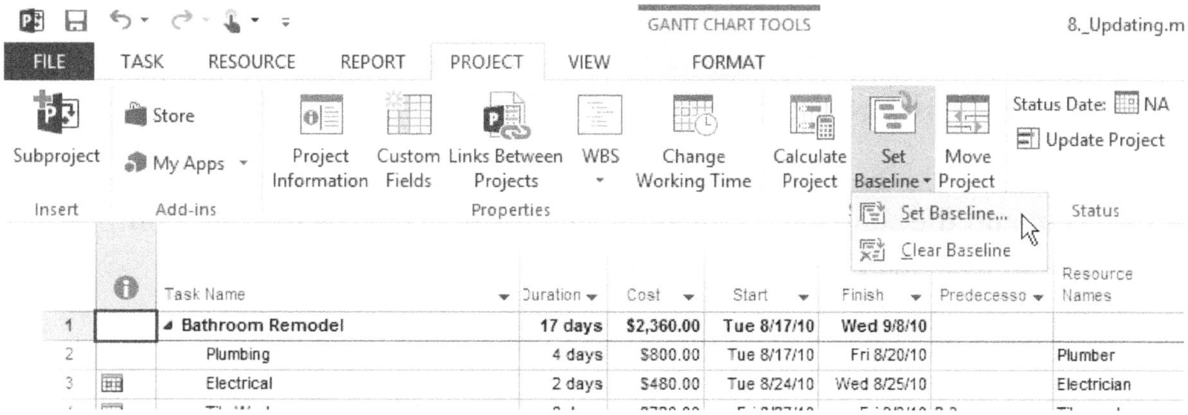


## Updating the Entire Project

Use the following procedure to update the entire project.

Step 1: If you want to update only certain tasks, select them from the Gantt chart view first.

Step 2: On the **Project** Tab select **Update Project**.

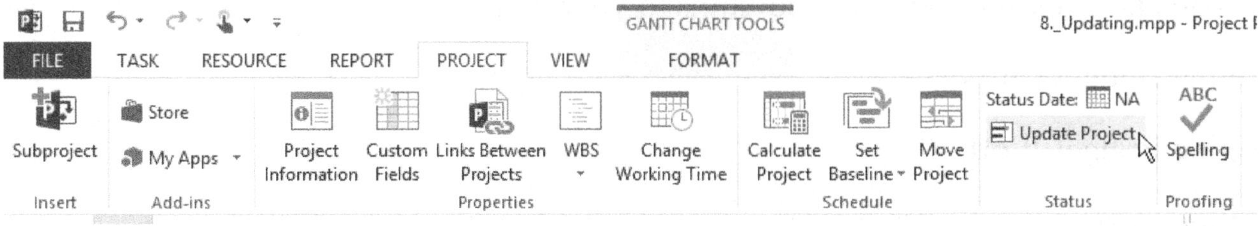


Project displays the *Update Project* dialog box.

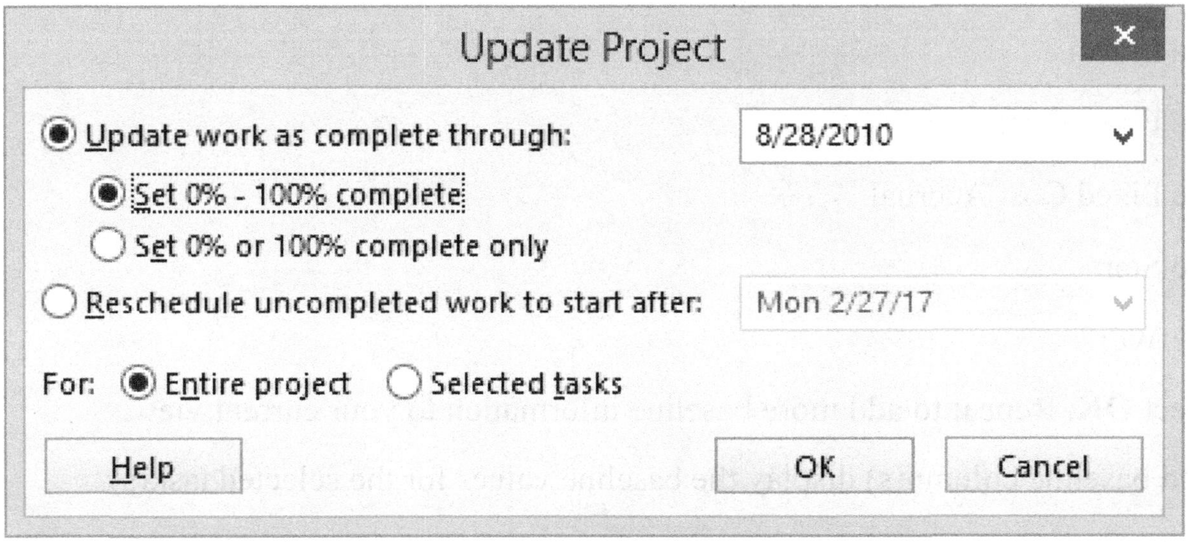


Step 3: Leave the default setting of **Update work as complete through**. Select the date (for this example, use 8/28/10) from the drop down calendar.

Step 4: Select **Set 0% - 100% complete** to have project indicate the percentage complete based on the duration and the schedule. To have Project set any tasks that are complete to 100%, and all others to 0%, select Set 0% or 100% complete only.

Step 5: Select **Entire project** or **Selected tasks**.

Step 6: Select **OK**.

Project updates the schedule and displays the Percent Complete on the Gantt Chart view. Any completed tasks now have a task completed icon in the Indicators column.

## Updating Task Actual Values

Use the following procedure to update the task actual values.

Step 1: Select the task you want to update. If multiple tasks have the same values, you can hold the CTRL key while you select multiple tasks.

Step 2: Select the **Task** tab from the Ribbon.

Step 3: Select the arrow next to **Mark on Track**. Select **Update Tasks**.

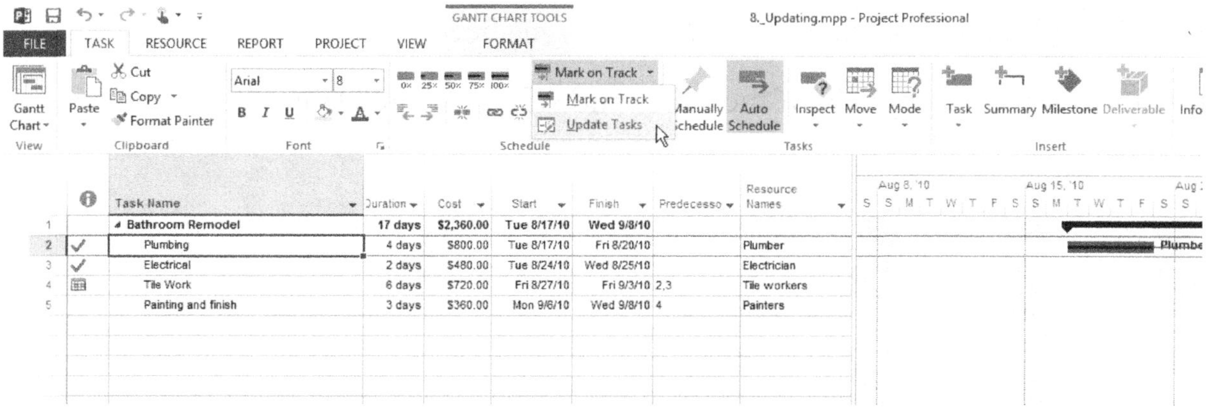


Project displays the *Update Tasks* dialog box.

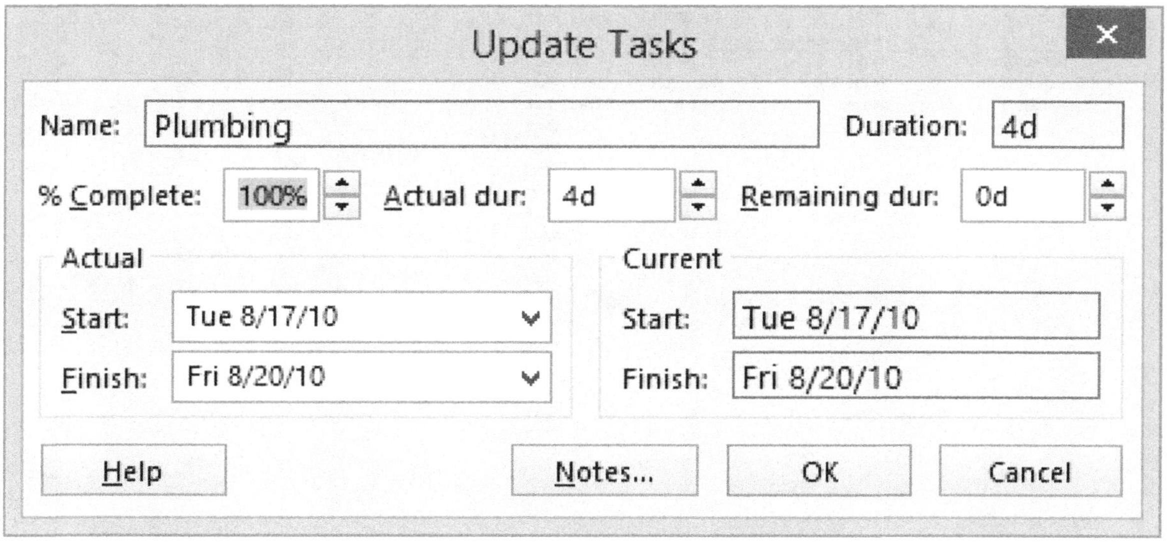


Step 4: Set the % **Complete** by entering the percentage or using the up and down arrows.

Step 5: Set the **Actual Duration** by entering the number and the duration abbreviation or by using the up and down arrows.

Step 6: Set the **Remaining Duration** by entering the number and duration abbreviation or by using the up and down arrows.

Step 7: Select the **Actual Start** date from the drop down calendar.

Step 8: Select the **Actual Finish** date from the drop down calendar.

Step 9: Select the **Notes** button to enter any notes about the task.

Step 10: Select **OK**.

## Updating Actual Work

To enter actual work.

Step 1: Select the **View** tab.

Step 2: Select **Task Usage** to switch to the *Task Usage* sheet.

Step 3: Right click on the right side of the sheet and select **Actual Work** from the context menu.

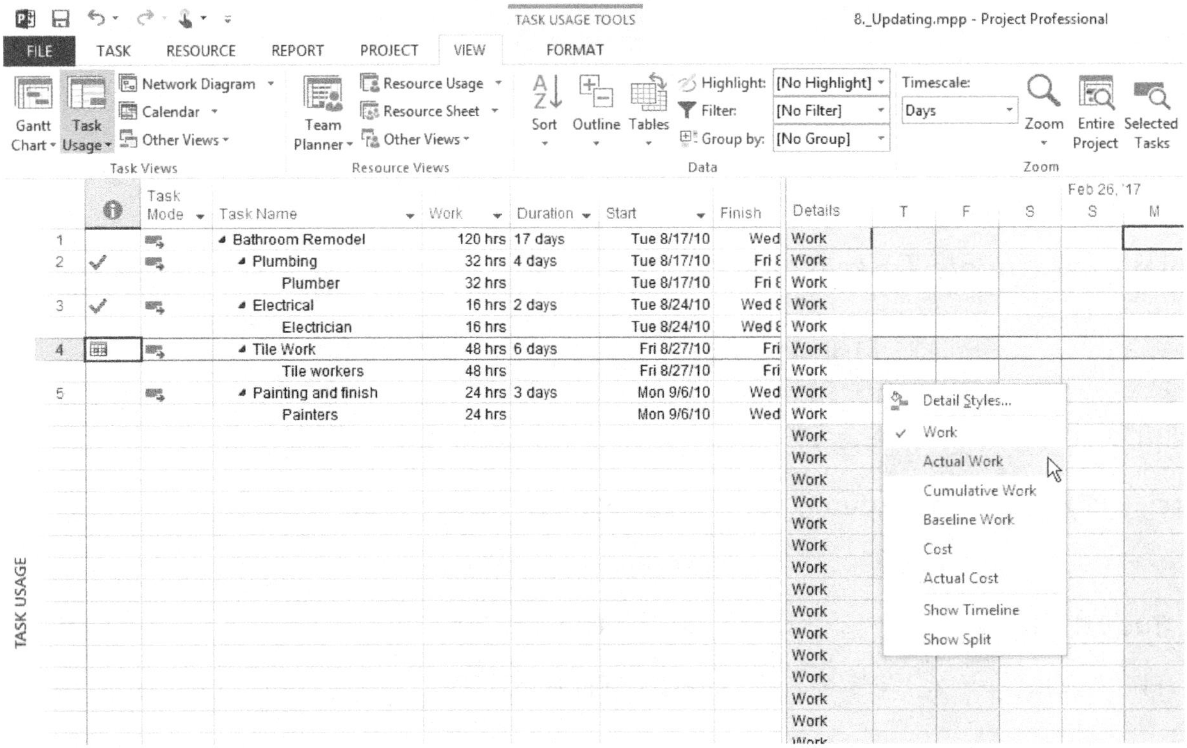

Step 4: Change the table for the Task Usage sheet by selecting **Table** from the **View** tab. Select **Work**.

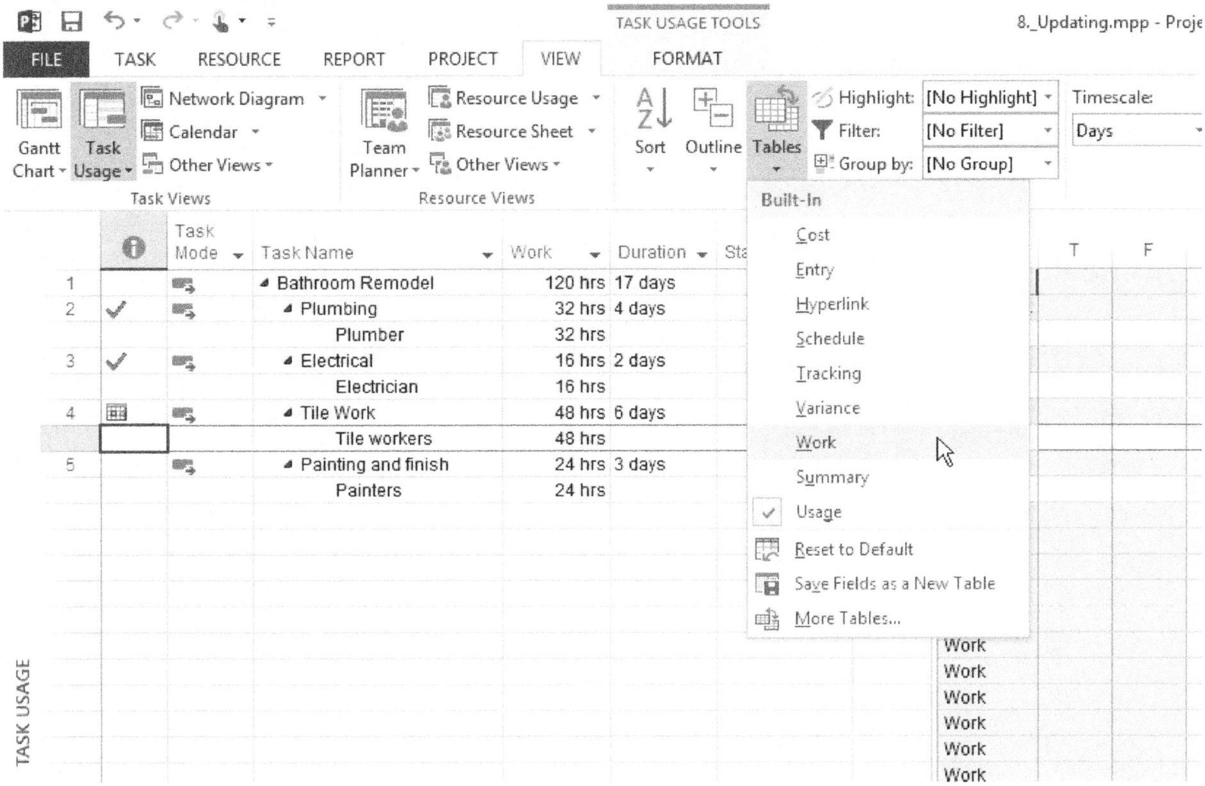


Step 5: Enter the actual work values in the appropriate dates on the right side of the sheet. You can also adjust the total actual work.

## Updating Actual Costs

Use the following procedure to turn off the automatic calculation of actual costs

Step 1: Select the File tab from the Ribbon.

Step 2: Select **Options**.

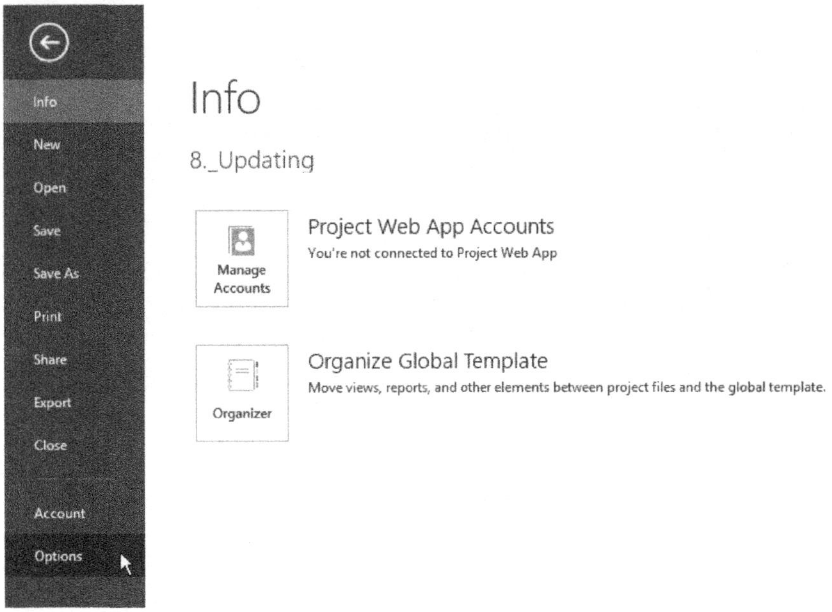


Project opens the *Project Options* dialog box.

Step 3: Select the **Schedule** tab.

Step 4: Clear the **Actual costs are always calculated by Project** box.

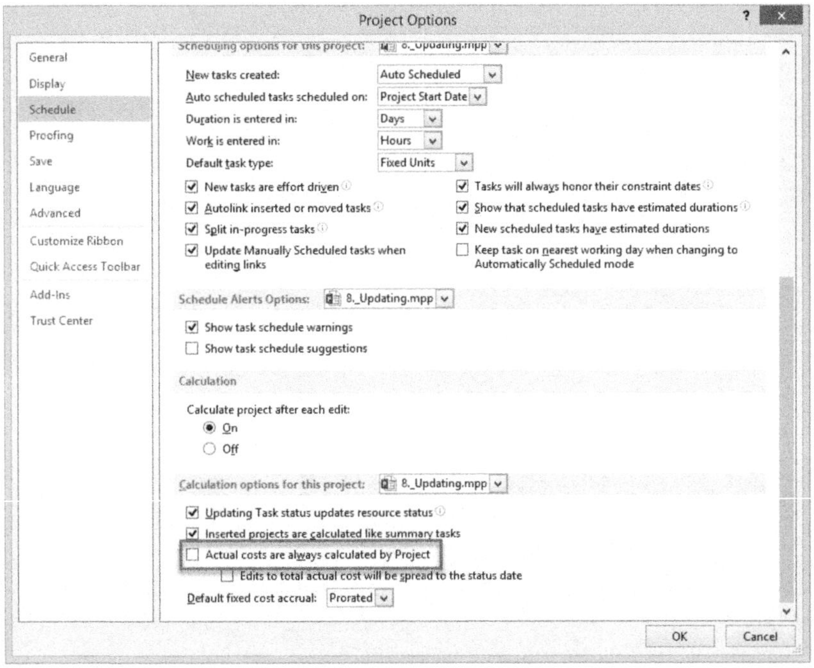

Entering actual costs.

Step 1: Select **Task Usage** from the **View** menu.

Step 2: Right click the right side of the sheet and select **Actual Cost** from the context menu.

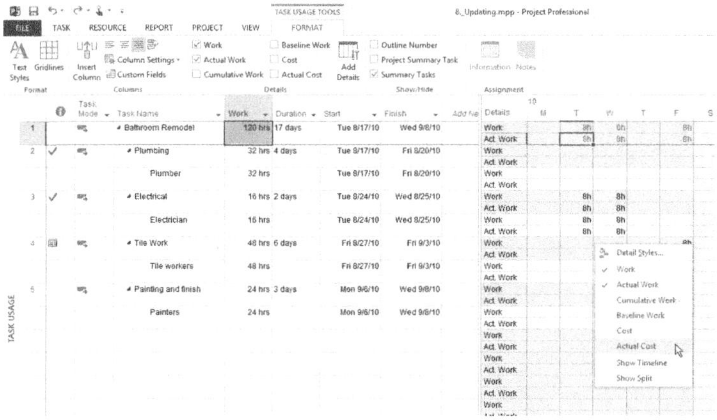


Step 3: Change the table for the Task Usage sheet by selecting **Table** from the **View** menu. Select **Tracking.**

Step 4: Enter the actual cost values in the appropriate dates on the right side of the sheet. You can also adjust the total actual cost. You may have to press TAB or scroll to see the Actual Cost column on the left side of the sheet.

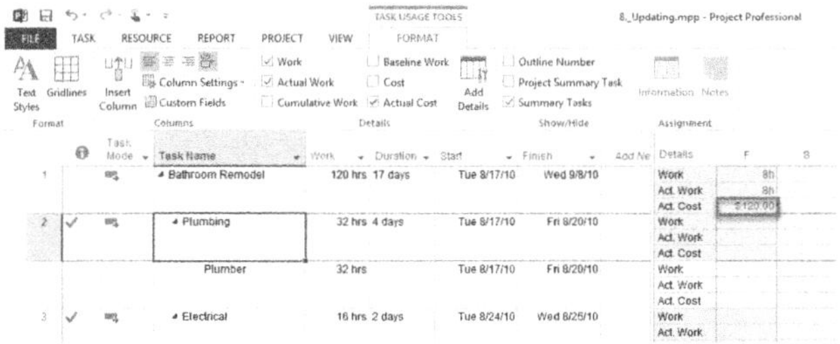

# Chapter 8 – Checking Project Progress

An important aspect of project management is checking on the project's progress and making adjustments in your plan where necessary. This chapter will explain how to view project statistics and costs. It will also show you how to check variances in work or cost. You will also learn how to identify slipped tasks and save an interim plan.

## Viewing Project Statistics

Use the following procedure to review the project statistics.

Step 1: Select the **Project** tab.

Step 2: Select **Project Information**.

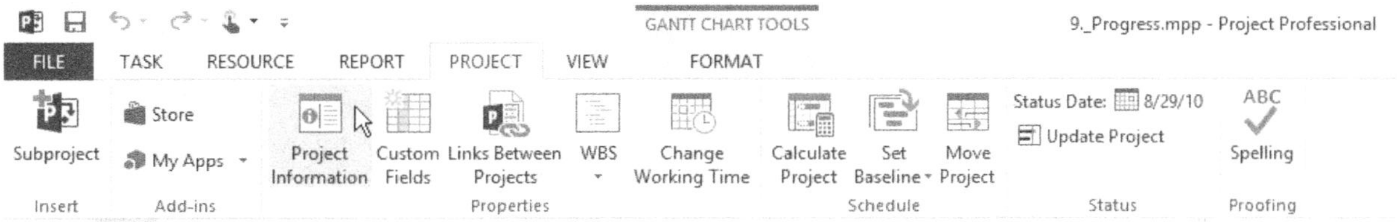


Project opens the *Project Information* dialog box.

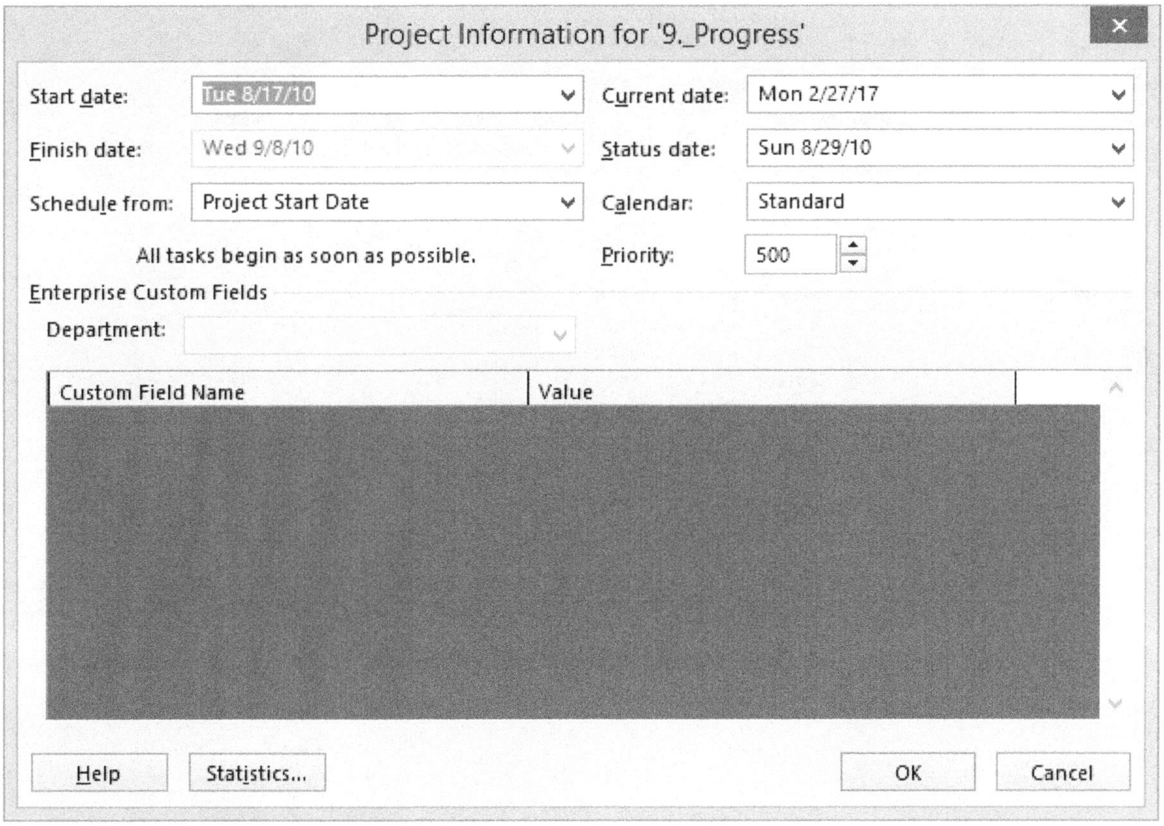


Step 3: Select the **Statistics** button.

Project displays the *Project Statistics* dialog box.

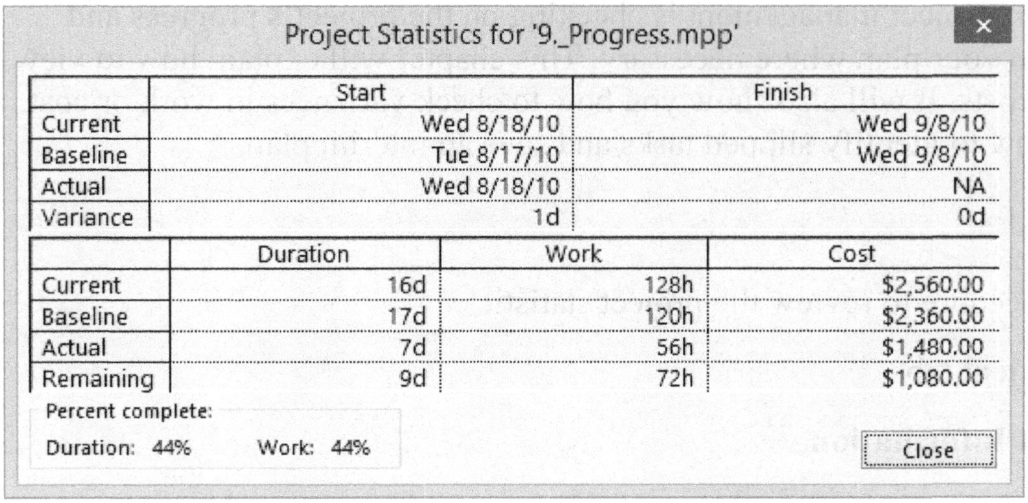

Project Statistics for '9._Progress.mpp'

| | Start | Finish |
|---|---|---|
| Current | Wed 8/18/10 | Wed 9/8/10 |
| Baseline | Tue 8/17/10 | Wed 9/8/10 |
| Actual | Wed 8/18/10 | NA |
| Variance | 1d | 0d |

| | Duration | Work | Cost |
|---|---|---|---|
| Current | 16d | 128h | $2,560.00 |
| Baseline | 17d | 120h | $2,360.00 |
| Actual | 7d | 56h | $1,480.00 |
| Remaining | 9d | 72h | $1,080.00 |

Percent complete:

Duration: 44% Work: 44%

Close

## Viewing Project Costs

Use the following procedure to switch to and view the Cost table.

Step 1: Starting from the Gantt Chart view, select **Tables** from the **View** tab. Select **Cost**.

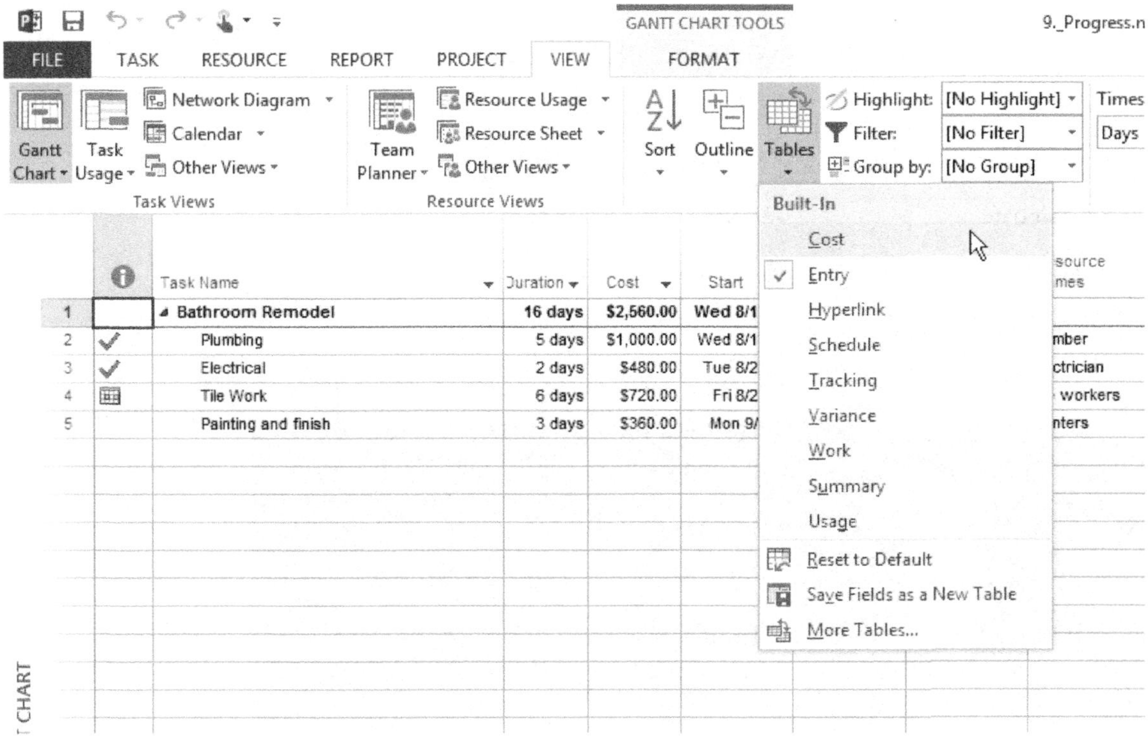

Step 2: Drag the divider to the right to see more of the Cost columns at one time.

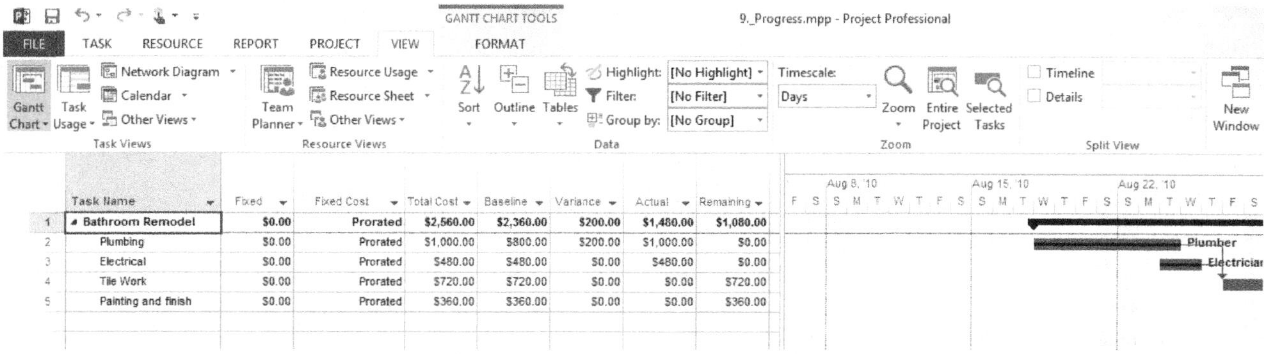


You can add columns to the current view. Discuss the different cost-related columns available beyond what is shown in the Cost table.

## Checking Duration Variance

Use the following procedure to check the duration variance.

Step 1: From the Gantt Chart view, right-click the **Duration** column and select **Insert Column** from the context menu.

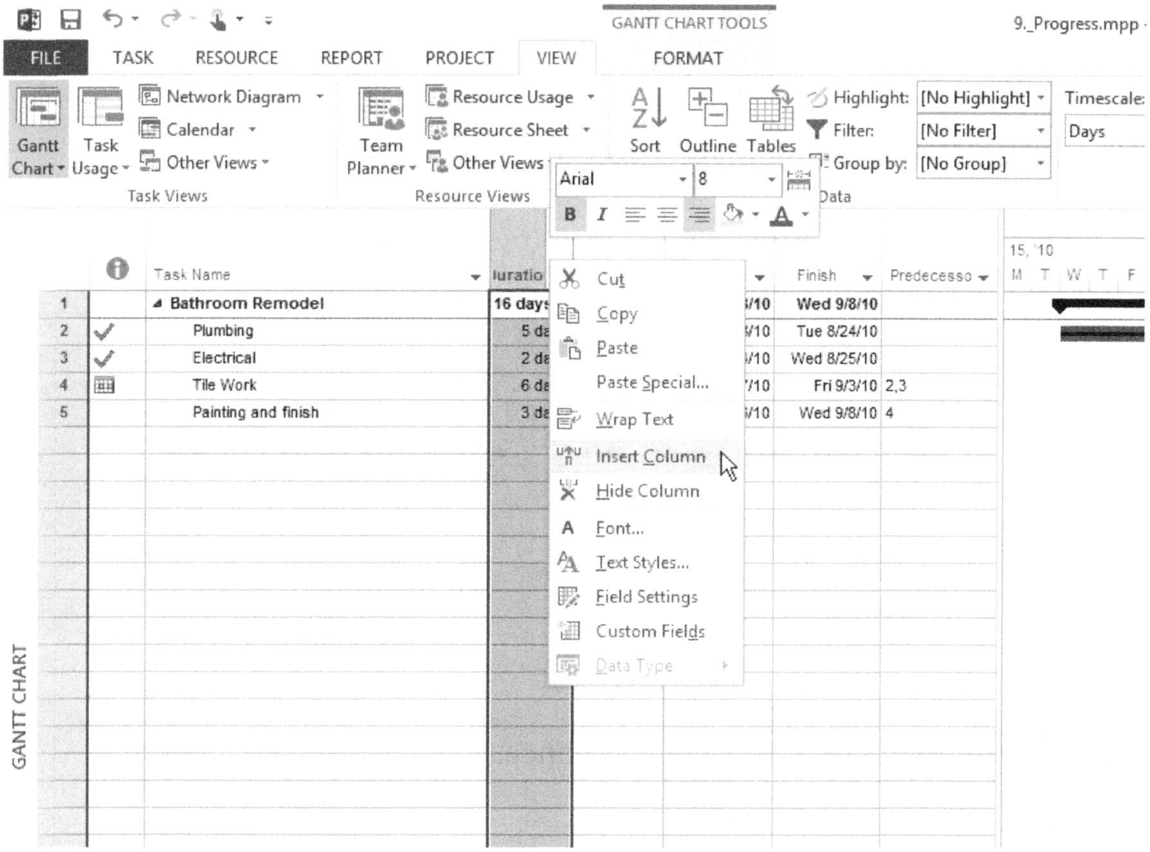

Step 2: Select **Duration Variance** as the **Field Name**.

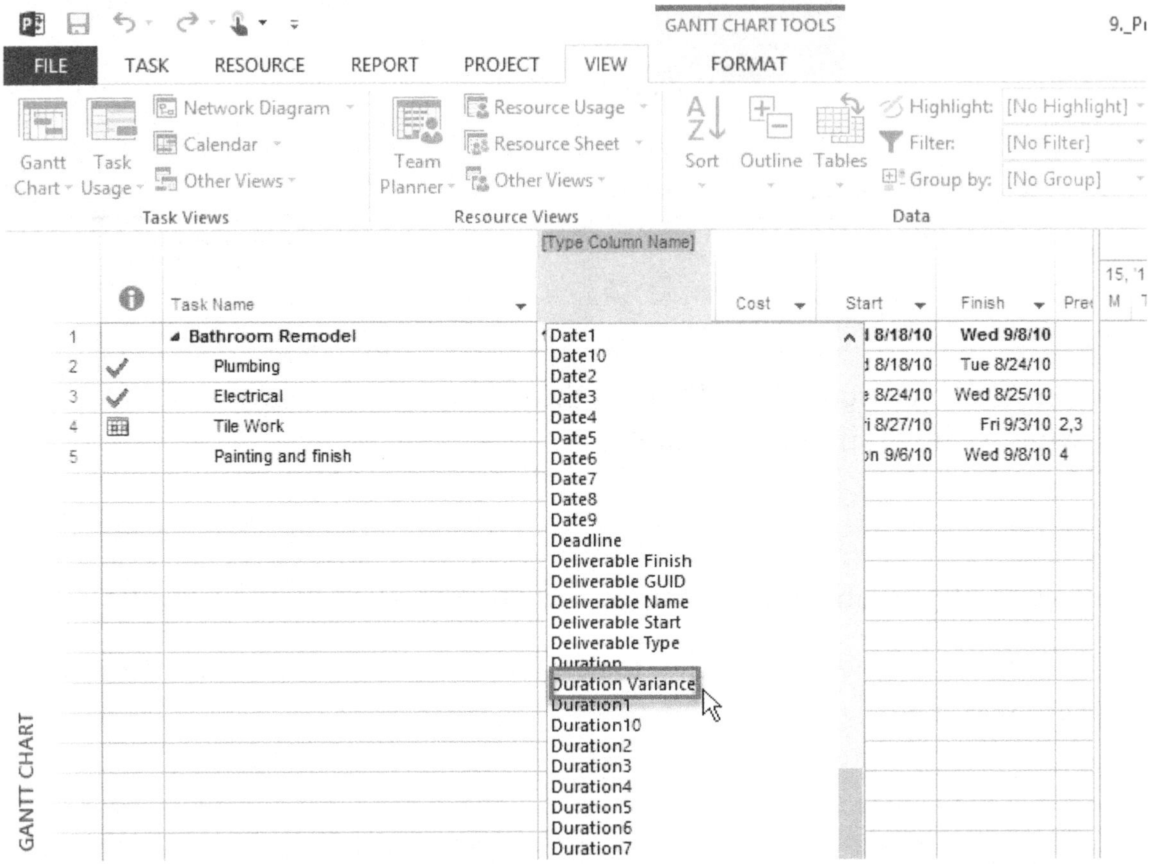


View the duration variance for the Summary Tasks and the detail tasks.

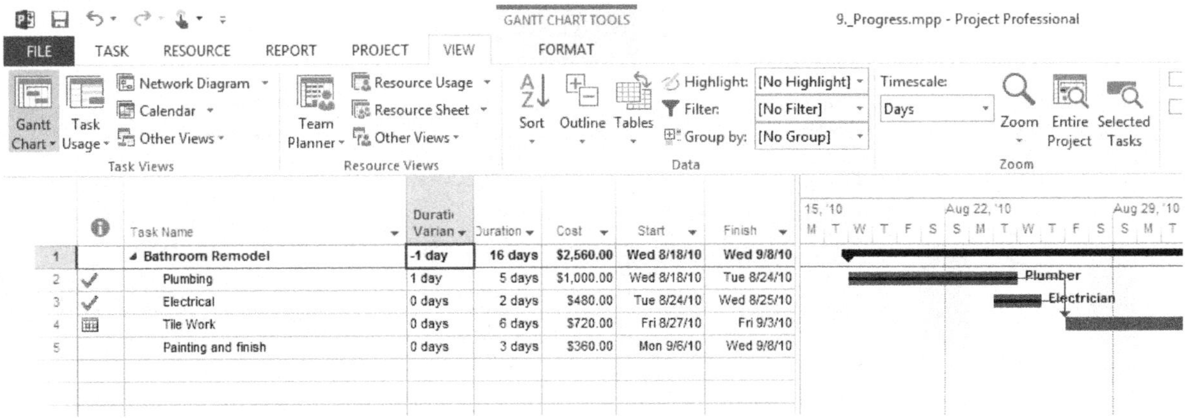


## Checking Work Variance

Use the following procedure to check the work variance.

Step 1: Select **Task Usage** from the **View** tab.

Step 2: Right-click one of the column headings and select **Insert Column** from the context menu.

Step 3: Select **Work Variance** as the **Field Name**.

View the work variance for the Summary Tasks and the detail tasks.

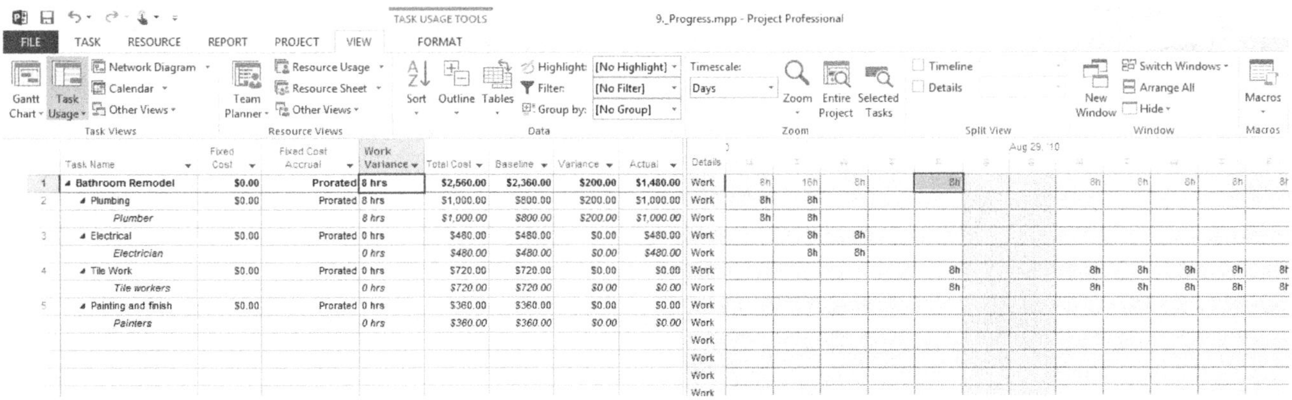

| | Task Name | Fixed Cost | Fixed Cost Accrual | Work Variance | Total Cost | Baseline | Variance | Actual | Details |
|---|---|---|---|---|---|---|---|---|---|
| 1 | Bathroom Remodel | $0.00 | Prorated | 8 hrs | $2,560.00 | $2,360.00 | $200.00 | $1,480.00 | Work |
| 2 | Plumbing | $0.00 | Prorated | 8 hrs | $1,000.00 | $800.00 | $200.00 | $1,000.00 | Work |
| | Plumber | | | 8 hrs | $1,000.00 | $800.00 | $200.00 | $1,000.00 | Work |
| 3 | Electrical | $0.00 | Prorated | 0 hrs | $480.00 | $480.00 | $0.00 | $480.00 | Work |
| | Electrician | | | 0 hrs | $480.00 | $480.00 | $0.00 | $480.00 | Work |
| 4 | Tile Work | $0.00 | Prorated | 0 hrs | $720.00 | $720.00 | $0.00 | $0.00 | Work |
| | Tile workers | | | 0 hrs | $720.00 | $720.00 | $0.00 | $0.00 | Work |
| 5 | Painting and finish | $0.00 | Prorated | 0 hrs | $360.00 | $360.00 | $0.00 | $0.00 | Work |
| | Painters | | | 0 hrs | $360.00 | $360.00 | $0.00 | $0.00 | Work |

## Checking Cost Variance

Use the following procedure to check the cost variance.

Step 1: Select **Tables** from the **View** tab. Select **Cost**.

View the cost variance for the Summary Tasks and the detail tasks.

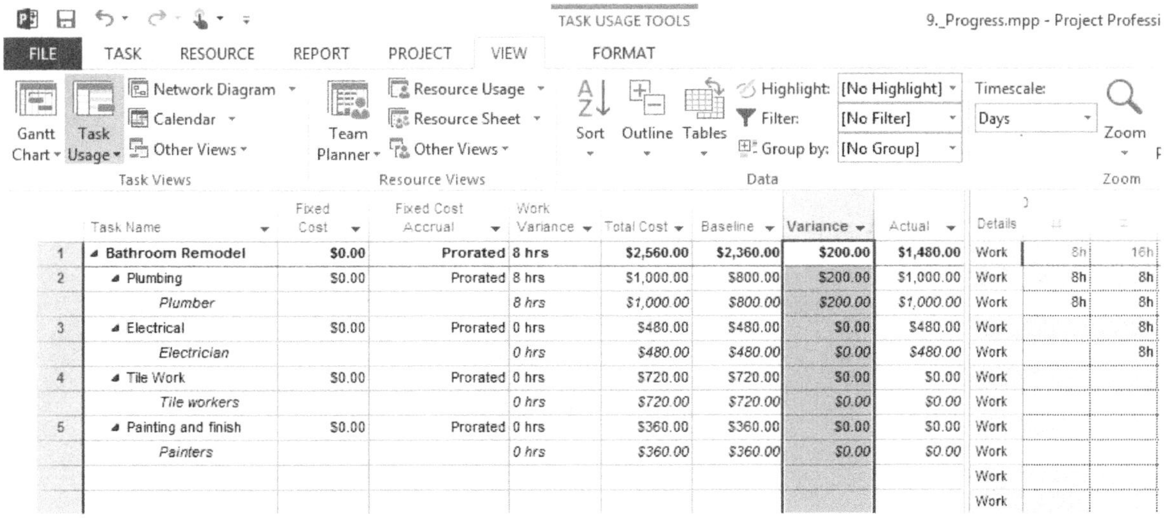

| | Task Name | Fixed Cost | Fixed Cost Accrual | Work Variance | Total Cost | Baseline | Variance | Actual | Details | | |
|---|---|---|---|---|---|---|---|---|---|---|---|
| 1 | Bathroom Remodel | $0.00 | Prorated | 8 hrs | $2,560.00 | $2,360.00 | $200.00 | $1,480.00 | Work | 8h | 16h |
| 2 | Plumbing | $0.00 | Prorated | 8 hrs | $1,000.00 | $800.00 | $200.00 | $1,000.00 | Work | 8h | 8h |
| | Plumber | | | 8 hrs | $1,000.00 | $800.00 | $200.00 | $1,000.00 | Work | 8h | 8h |
| 3 | Electrical | $0.00 | Prorated | 0 hrs | $480.00 | $480.00 | $0.00 | $480.00 | Work | | 8h |
| | Electrician | | | 0 hrs | $480.00 | $480.00 | $0.00 | $480.00 | Work | | 8h |
| 4 | Tile Work | $0.00 | Prorated | 0 hrs | $720.00 | $720.00 | $0.00 | $0.00 | Work | | |
| | Tile workers | | | 0 hrs | $720.00 | $720.00 | $0.00 | $0.00 | Work | | |
| 5 | Painting and finish | $0.00 | Prorated | 0 hrs | $360.00 | $360.00 | $0.00 | $0.00 | Work | | |
| | Painters | | | 0 hrs | $360.00 | $360.00 | $0.00 | $0.00 | Work | | |

## Identifying Slipped Tasks

To check the work variance.

Step 1: Select the arrow next to **Gantt Chart** on the **View** tab. Select **Tracking Gantt**.

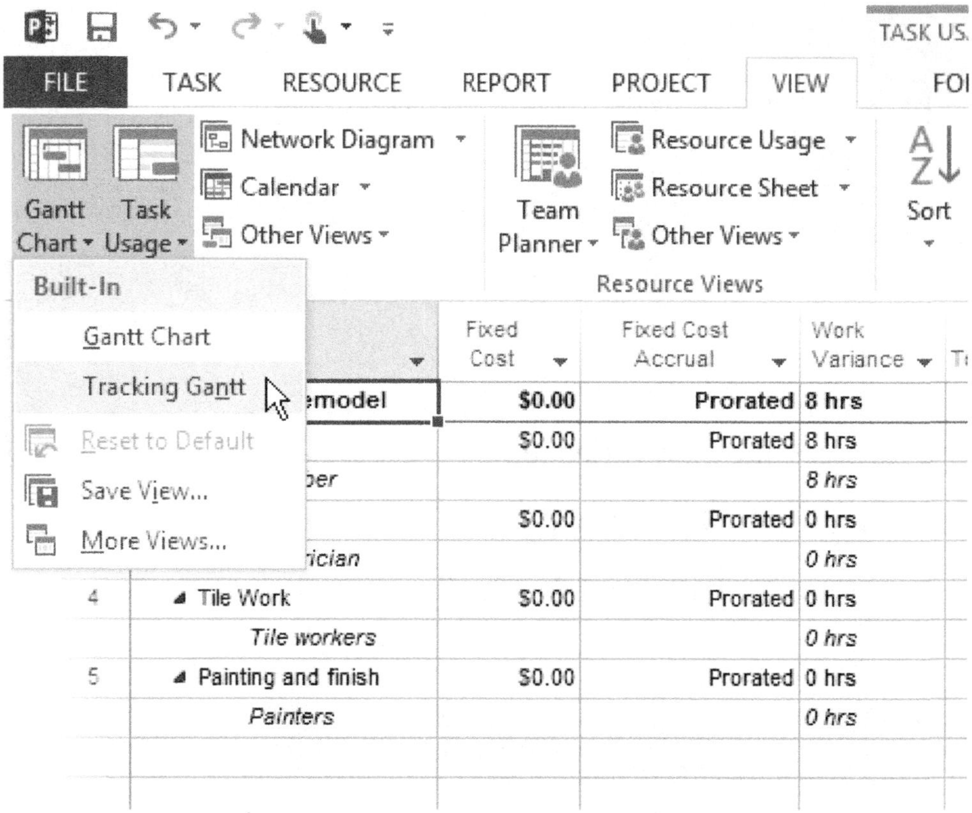

Step 2: Select **Tables** from the **View** tab. Select **Variance**.

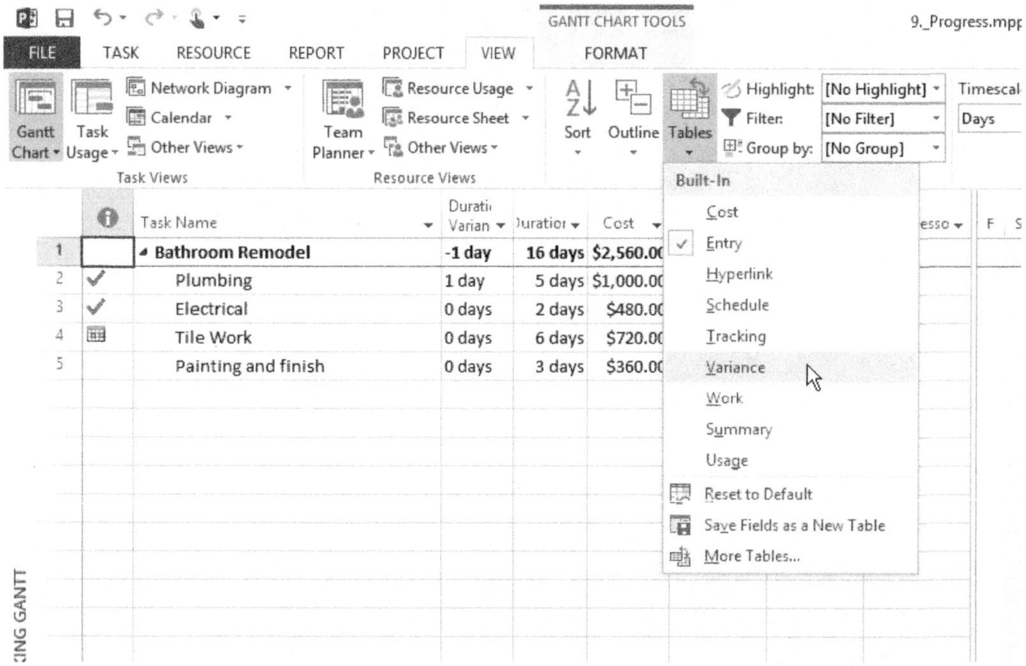

Step 3: Select **Filter** from the **View** tab. Select **More Filters**.

Step 4: Select **Slipping Tasks** and select **Apply**.

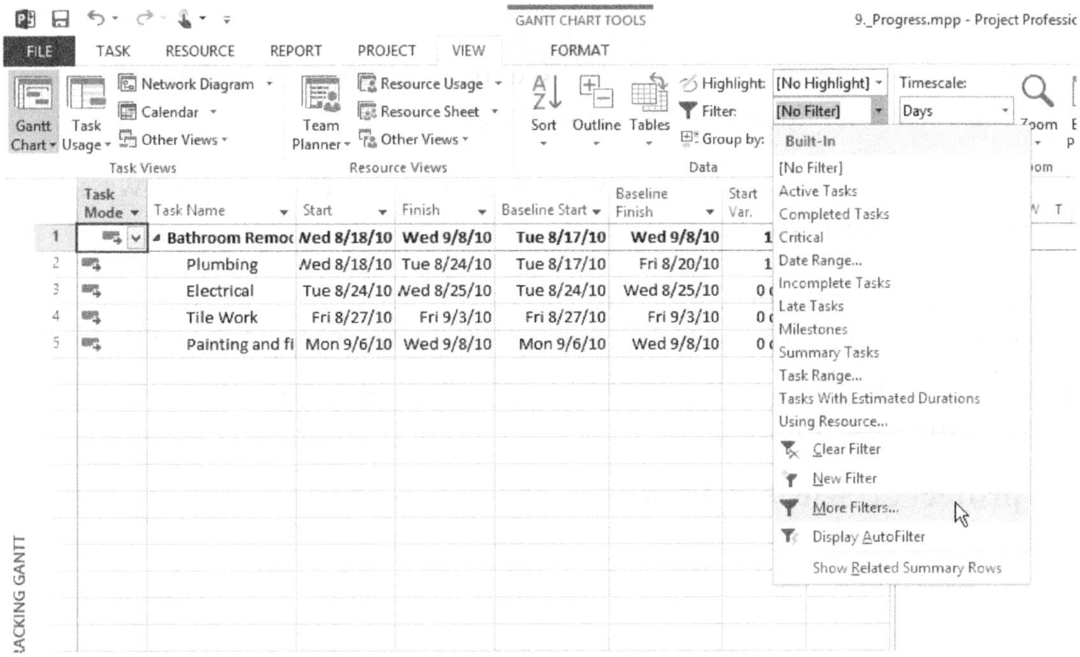


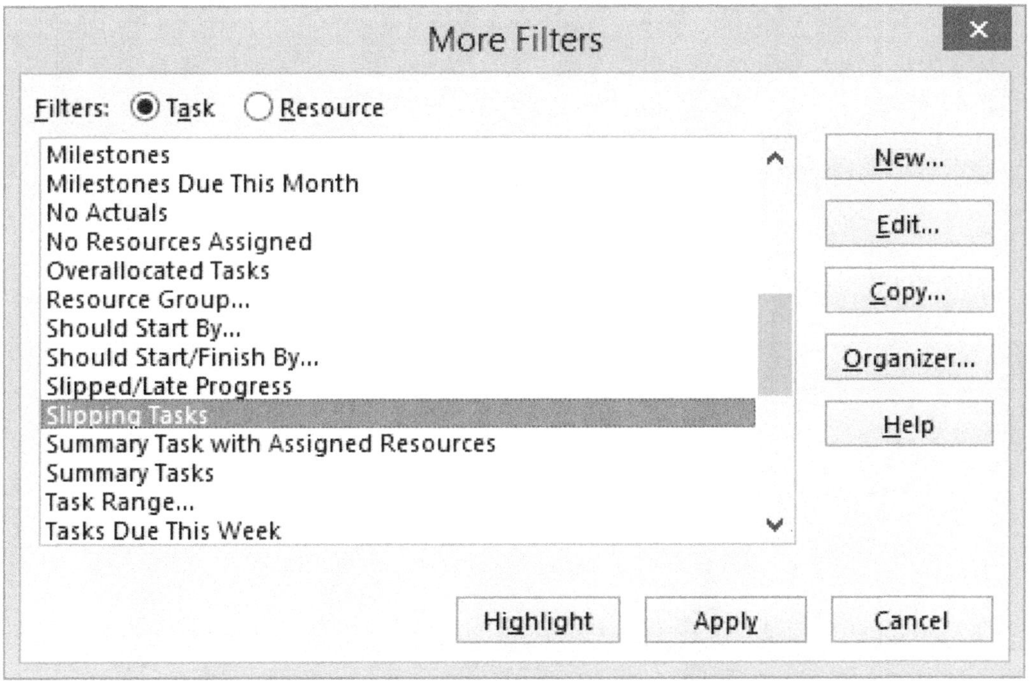


## Saving an Interim Plan

Setting an interim plan.

Step 1: Select **Set Baseline** from the **Project** tab.

Step 2: Select **Set Interim Plan**.

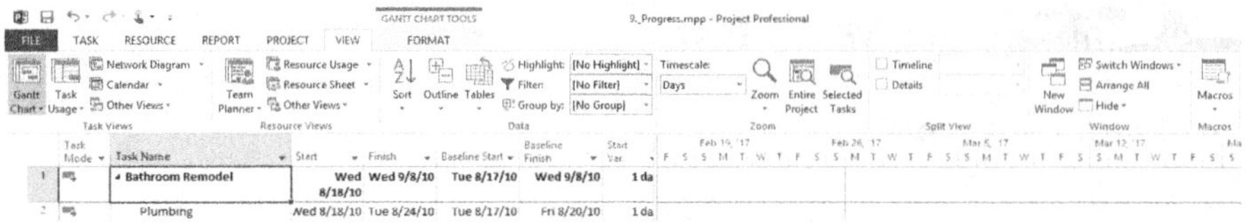

Step 3: Select a value that you want to save from the **Copy** drop down list. The current start date, finish date, and baseline values are not numbered.

Step 4: Select a value into which you want to copy values from the **Into** drop down list. Interim plans are stored in the Start and Finish fields.

**Note:** If you select a baseline in both the Copy and the Into fields, you will save a baseline, rather than an interim plan. If you select a baseline in the Copy box, and a start and finish interim plan in the Into box, only the start date and finish date from the baseline will be copied to the interim plan.

Step 5: Select **Entire project** or **Selected Tasks**.

Step 6: Select **OK**.

## Chapter 9 – Working with Reports

In this chapter, you will learn how to work with reports. You will learn how to customize basic and visual reports. You will also learn how to create a custom report. Finally, you will learn how to sort a report.

### Customizing a Basic Report

Use the following procedure to define the report contents.

Step 1: Select the **Project** tab from the Ribbon.

Step 2: Select **Reports**.

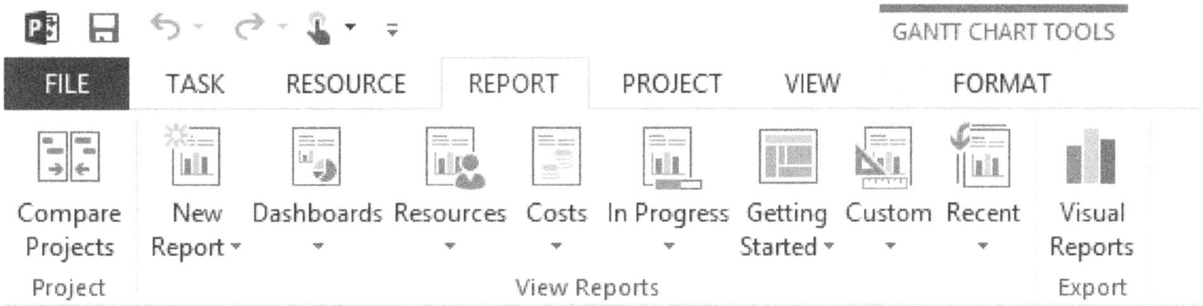


Step 3: Select **Current** and choose the **Select** button.

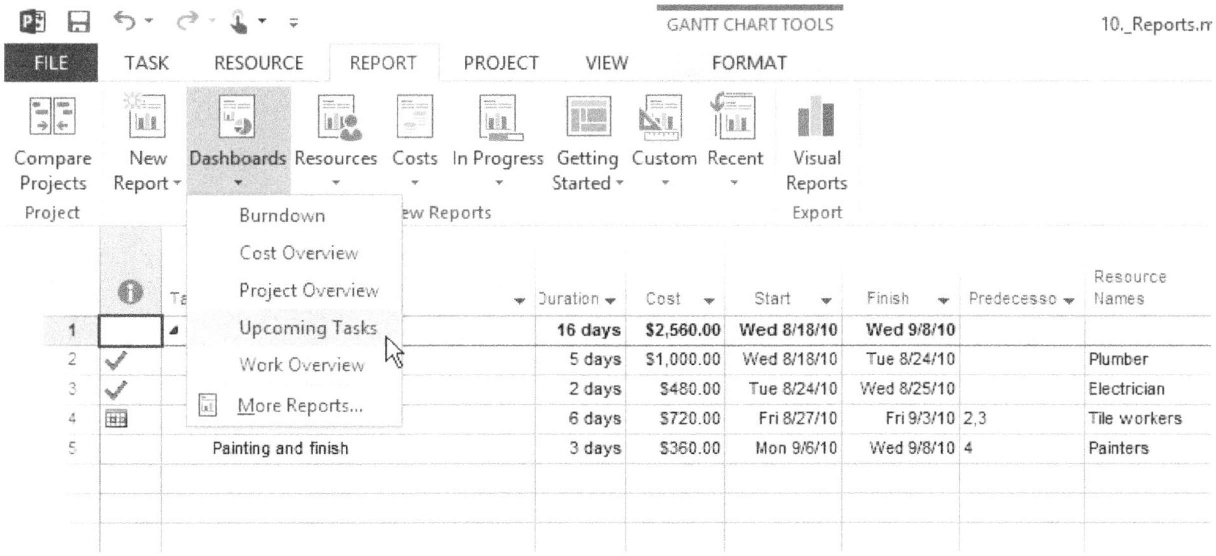

Step 4: Select **Tasks Starting Soon** and choose the **Edit** button.

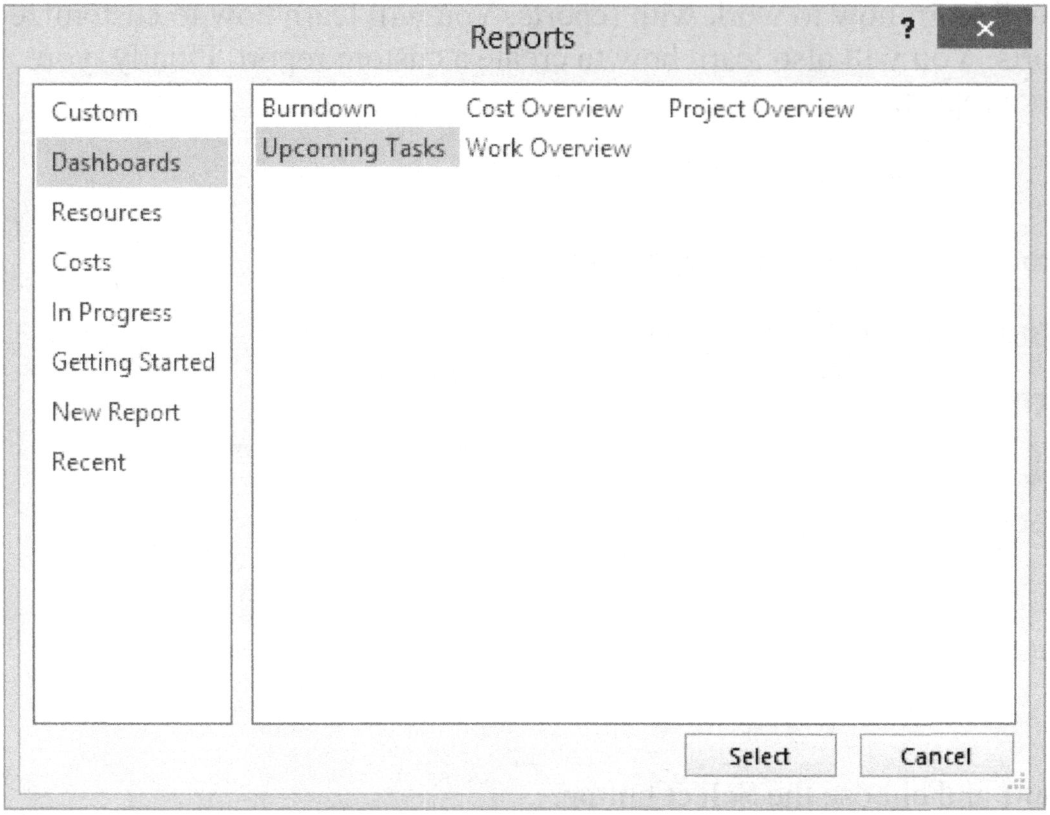


Step 5: Select the **Definition** tab.

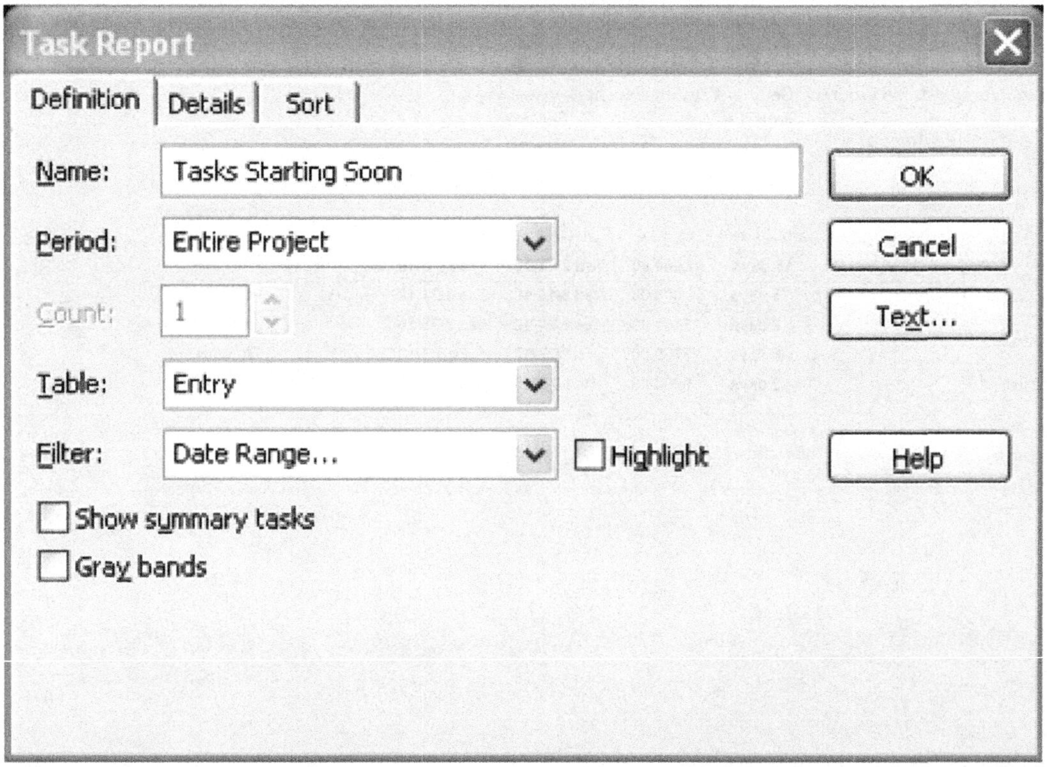


Step 6: Enter the **Name** for the report.

Step 7: Select the time **Period** for the report from the drop down list.

Step 8: If you select a time period other than the Entire Project, also select the **Count** (for example, 1 week).

Step 9: Select the **Table** from the drop down list to use as a base for the report.

Step 10: Select a **Filter** from the drop down list. Check the **Highlight** box if desired.

Step 11: Check the **Show Summary Tasks** box to show summary tasks on the report.

Step 12: Check the **Gray bands** box to show gray bands on the report as dividers.

Step 13: Select the **Text** button to format the report font style, size, and color.

Step 14: Select the **Details** tab.

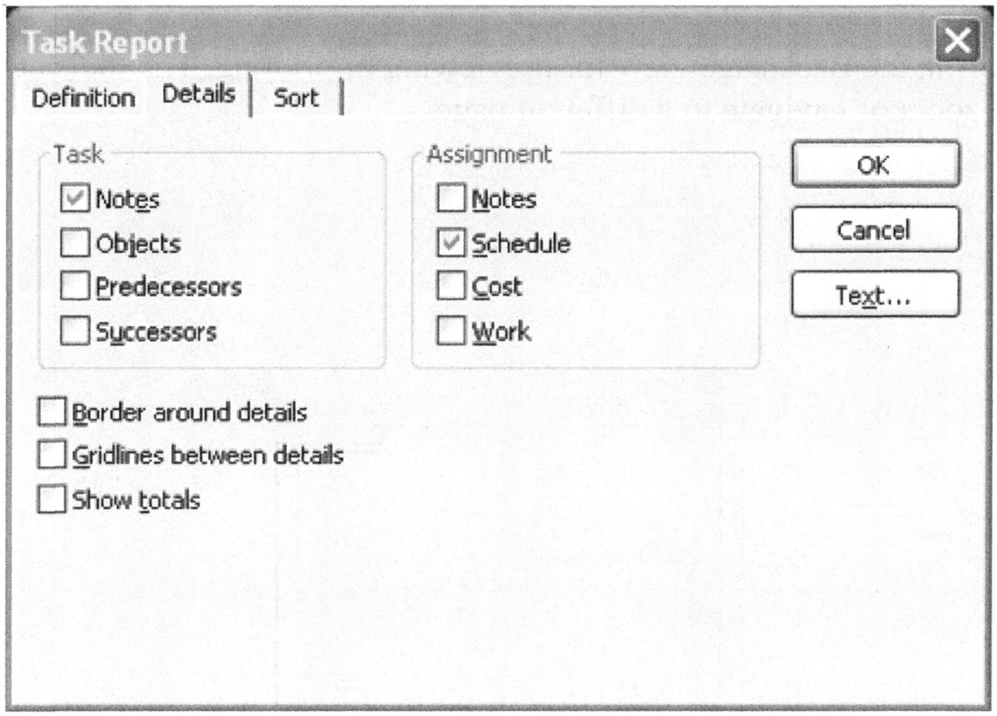


Step 15: Check the items that you would like to include on the report.

Step 16: Select **OK**.

Step 17: Now, in the *Current Activity Reports* window, choose the **Select** button to re-open the report.

## Creating a Custom Report

Selecting a custom report.

Step 1: Select the **Report** tab from the Ribbon.

Step 2: Select **Dashboard**.

Step 3: Select **Custom** and choose the **Select** button.

Step 4: Select an option from the **Custom Reports** list. Choose the **Select** button to run the report. Select the **New** or **Edit** to change the report definition (as in the previous topic).

Project displays the report in the Backstage view for previewing or printing. The tools at the bottom allow you to zoom or navigate to a different page.

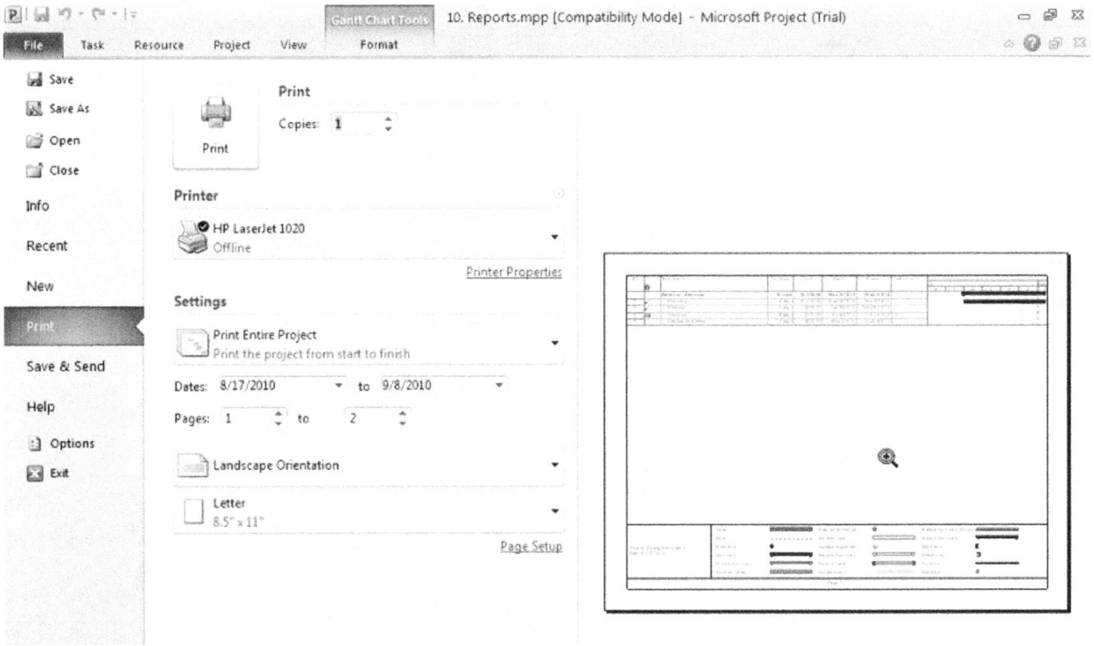


The Reports Organizer.

Step 1: Select the **Report** tab from the Ribbon.

Step 3: Select **Manage**.

Step 4: Select the **Organizer** button.

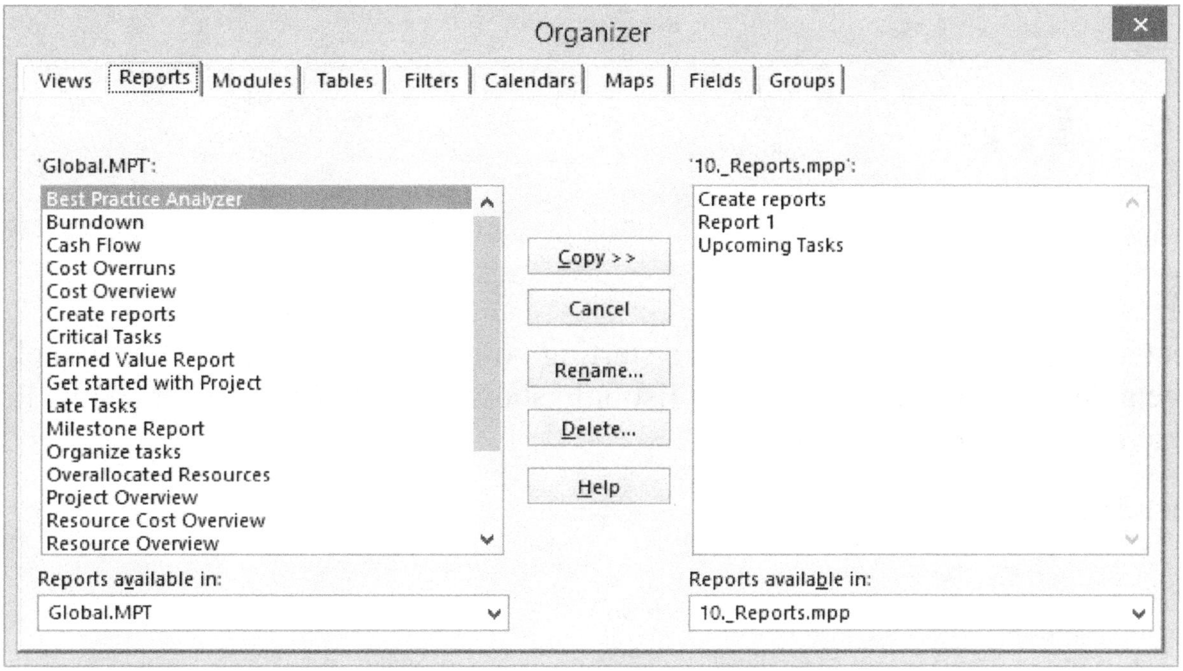


The left side of the dialog box lists available reports. You can select a different Project file from the drop down list (it must be open). The right side of the dialog box lists reports that are in your current project. To copy a report, highlight it on the left side and select **Copy**.

## Customizing a Visual Report

Use the following procedure to customize a visual report.

Step 1: Select the **Project** tab from the Ribbon.

Step 2: Select **Visual Reports**.

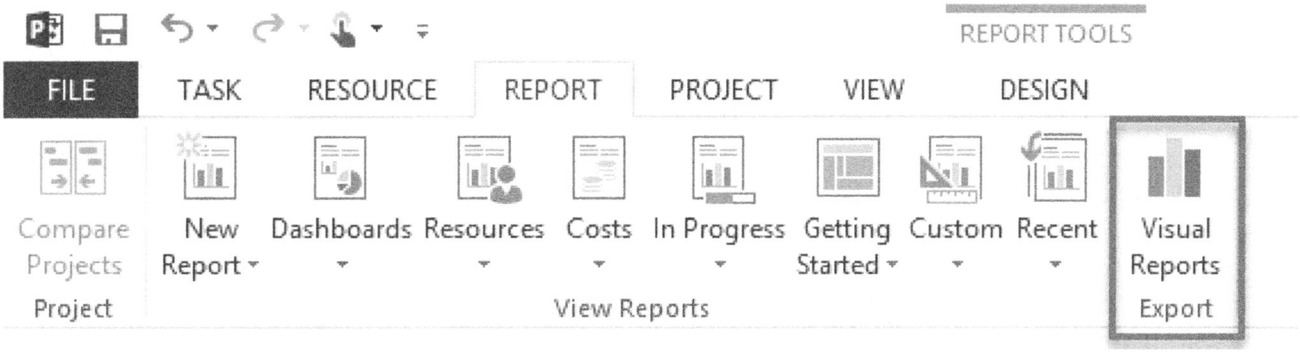

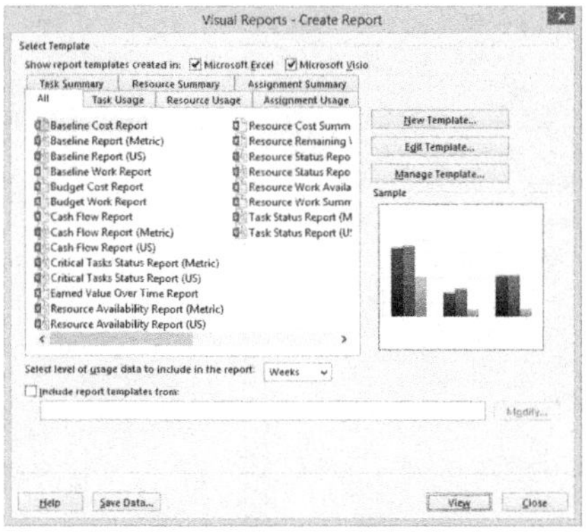


Step 3: Select a report from the list to use as a starting point. You must have either Excel or Visio to be able to run visual reports. The list only shows reports you have available if you do not have both programs installed.

Step 4: Select **Edit Template**.

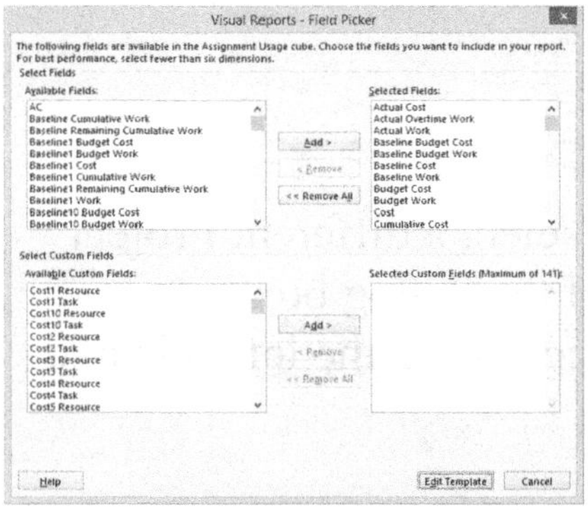


Step 5: In the **Selected Fields** column on the right, highlight fields you do not want included and select **Remove**. In the **Available Fields** column on the left, highlight the fields you do want to include on the report and select **Add**. For best report, include six or fewer fields in the report.

Step 6: Select **Edit Template**.

Step 7: The selected report opens in either Excel or Visio, depending on your selections.

## Sorting a Report

Use the following procedure to sort a report.

Step 1: Select the **Report** tab from the Ribbon.

Step 2: Select **Current** and choose the **Select** button.

Step 3: Select **Tasks Starting Soon** and choose the **Edit** button.

Step 4: Select the **Sort** tab.

Step 5: For up to three sorting options, select the field from the drop down lists. Select **Ascending** or **Descending** for each field.

Step 6: Check the **Keep outline structure** box to keep the outline structure for the sorted tasks.

Step 7: Select **OK**.

Step 8: Now, in the Report options window, choose the **Select** button.

## Chapter 10 – Working with Multiple Projects

This chapter explains how to handle multiple projects. You will learn how to create links between projects. Since working with a single file is always faster if you can help it, this chapter will also explain how to consolidate projects. You will learn how to view multiple project critical paths and consolidated project statistics. Finally, this chapter explains how to create a resource pool.

### Inserting a Subproject

Use the following procedure to link a project in a master project

Step 1: In the blank project, from the **Gantt Chart** view, highlight the row where you want to insert the project.

Step 2: Select the **Project** tab.

Step 3: Select **Subproject**.

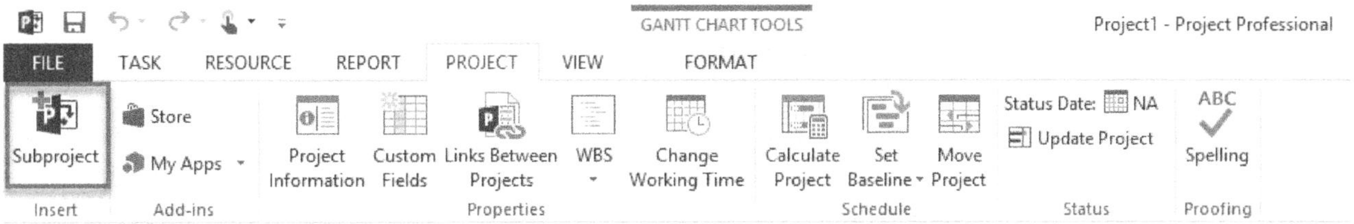


Step 4: Highlight the project you want to insert.

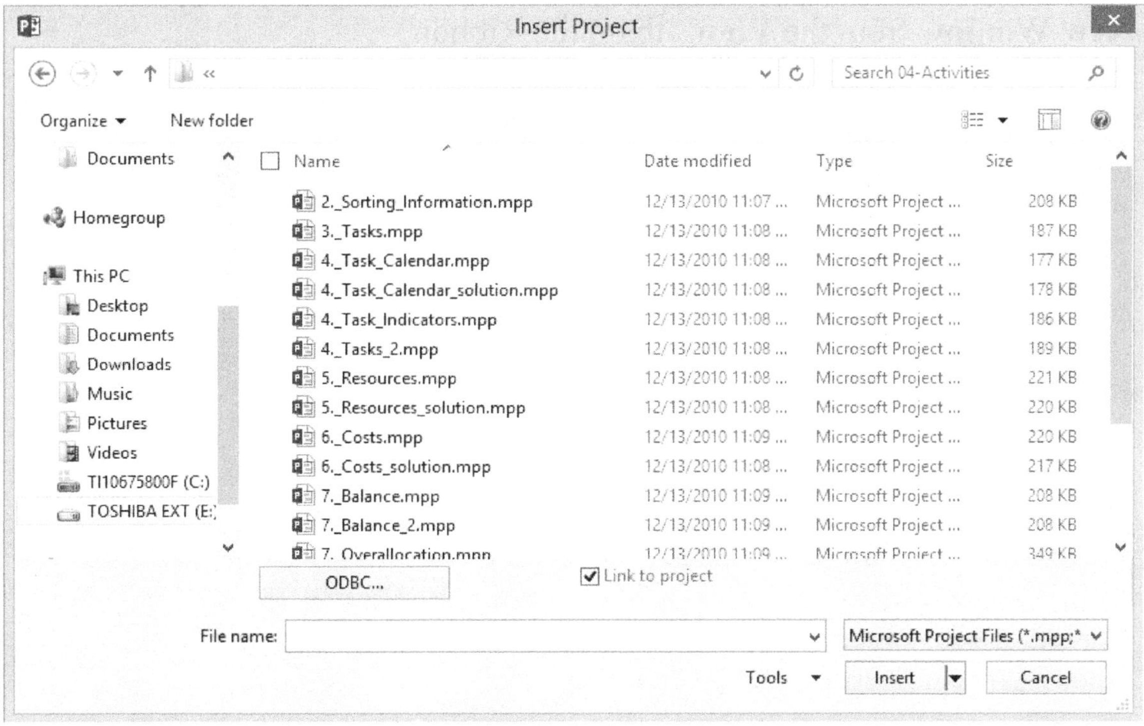

Note: To insert multiple projects, hold down CTRL and click the projects in the order that you want to insert them.

Step 5: Make sure the **Link to project** box is checked. However, if you do not want to update the subprojects with any changes made to the master project, clear the box.

Step 6: Select **Insert.**

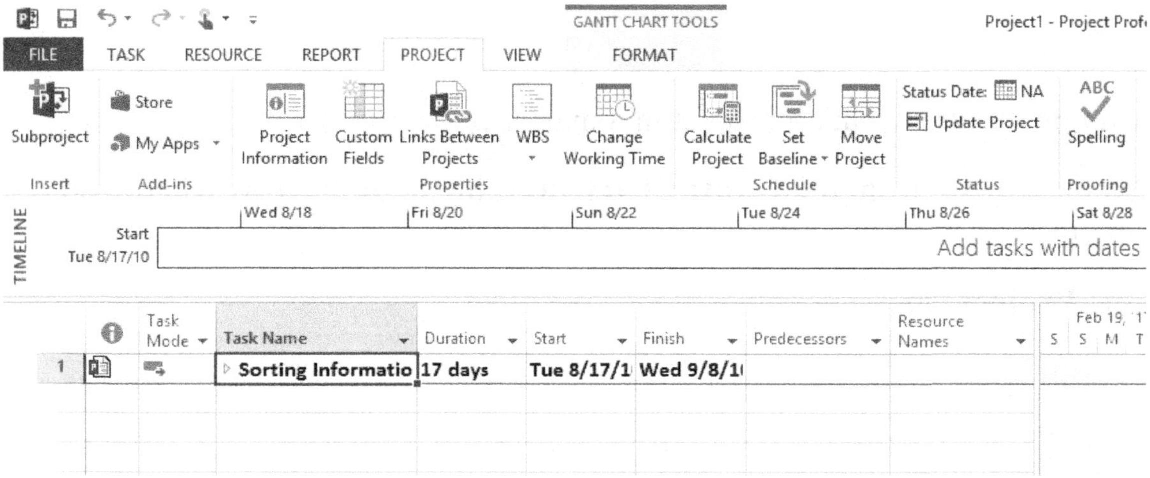


## Consolidating Projects

To consolidate projects for printing, use the following procedure.

Step 1: Open the project files you want to combine.

Step 2: Select **New Window** from the **View** tab on the Ribbon.

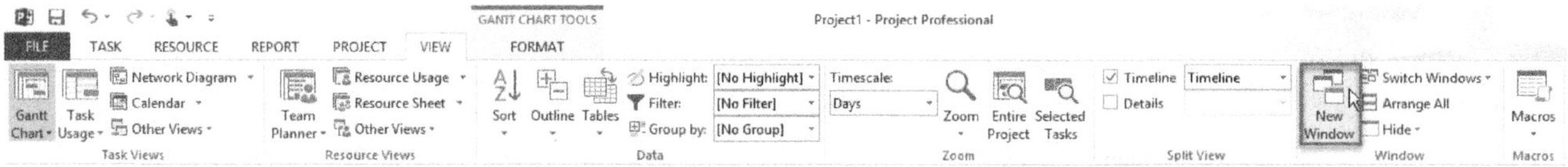

Step 3: Highlight the first file you want to appear in the consolidated window. Hold the CTRL key to select subsequent projects in the order you want them to appear.

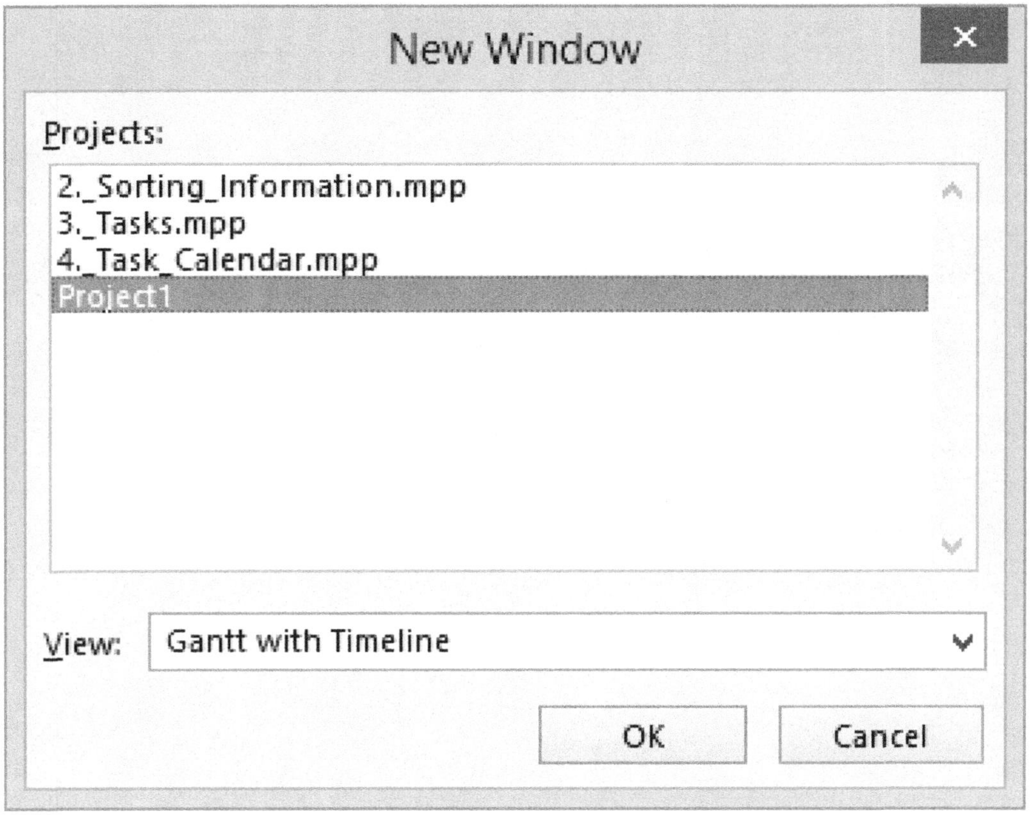


Step 4: Select a **View** option from the drop down list.

Step 5: Select **OK**.

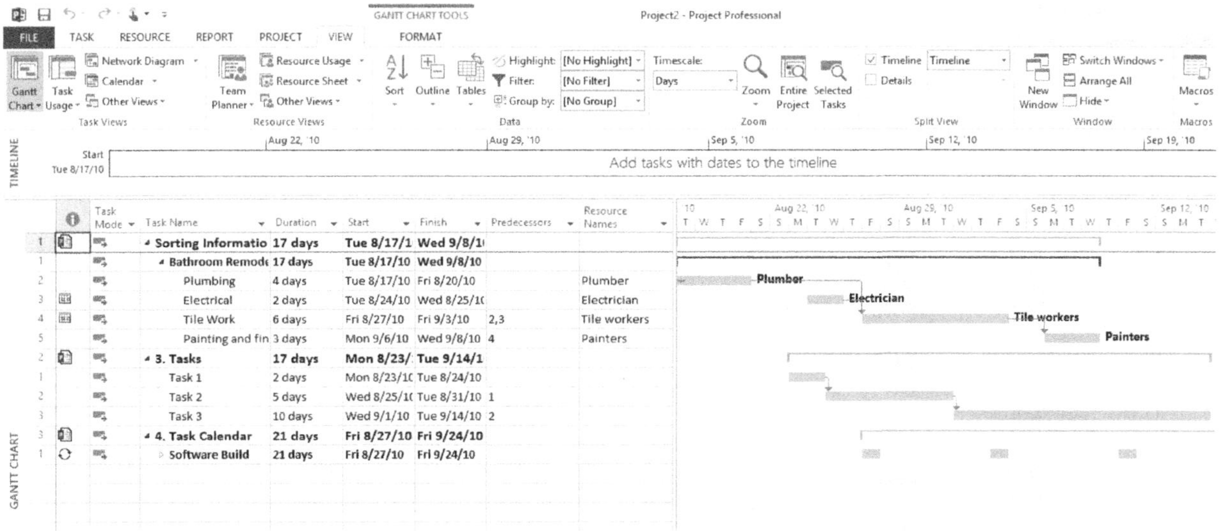


## Viewing Multiple Project Critical Paths

Use the following procedure to display multiple critical paths.

Step 1: Select the **File** tab from the Ribbon.

Step 2: Select **Options**.

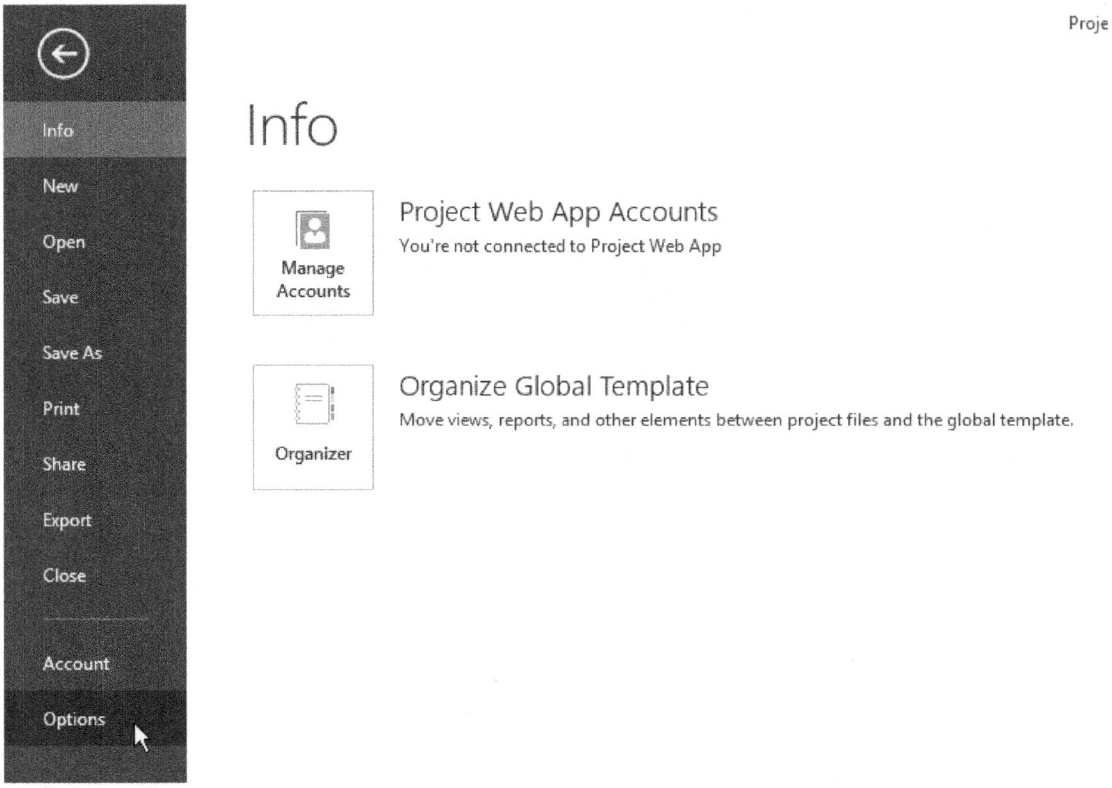


Project opens the *Project Options* dialog box.

Step 1: Select the **Advanced** tab.

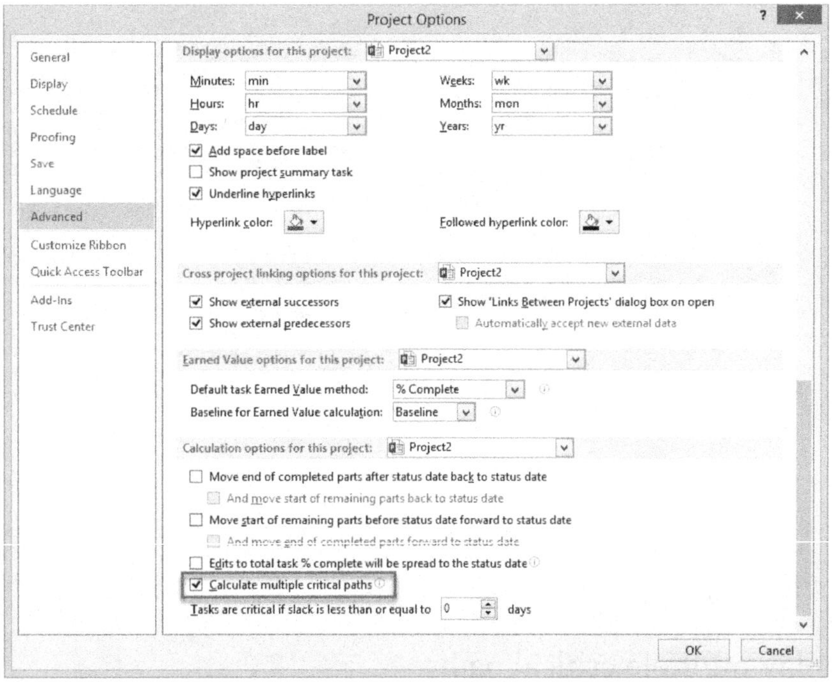

Step 2: Check the **Calculate Multiple Critical paths** box.

Step 3: Select **OK**.

Step 4: Select **More Views** from the **View** menu.

Step 5: Select **Detail Gantt**.

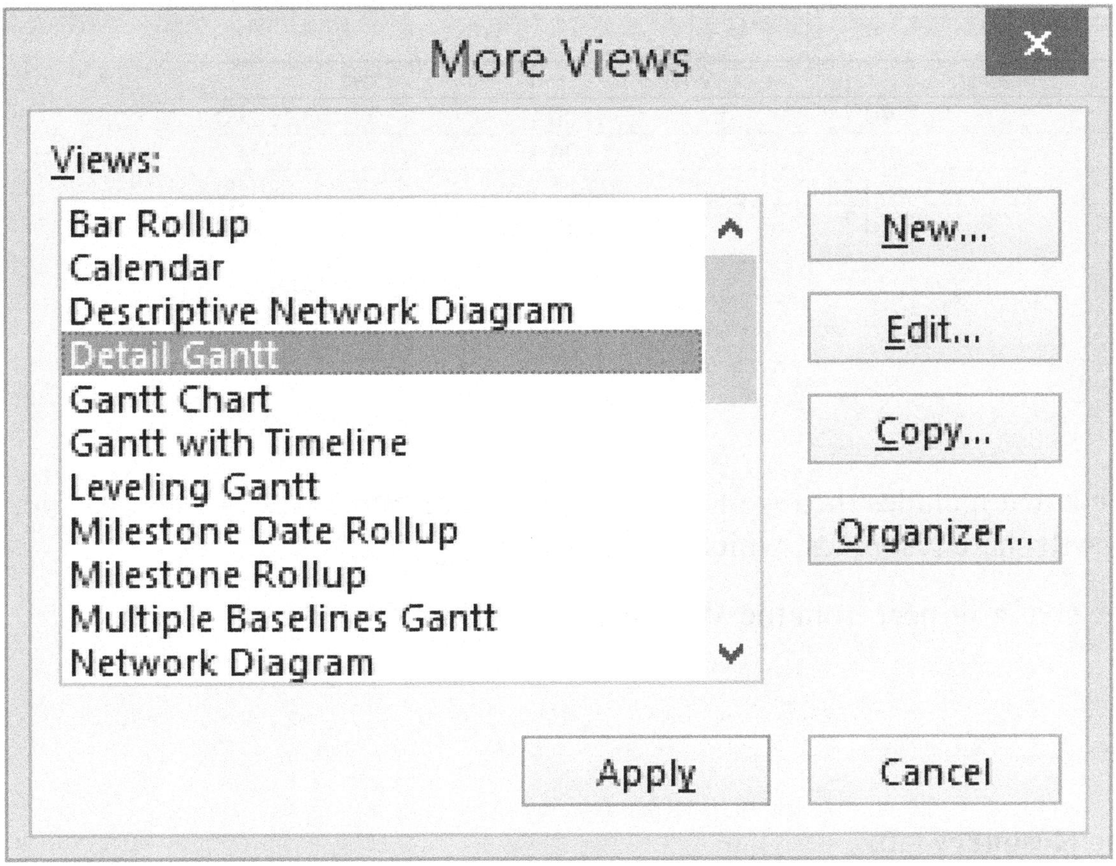


Step 6: Select **Apply**.

## Viewing Consolidated Project Statistics

Use the following procedure to review the project statistics.

Step 1: Select **Project Information** from the **Project** tab.

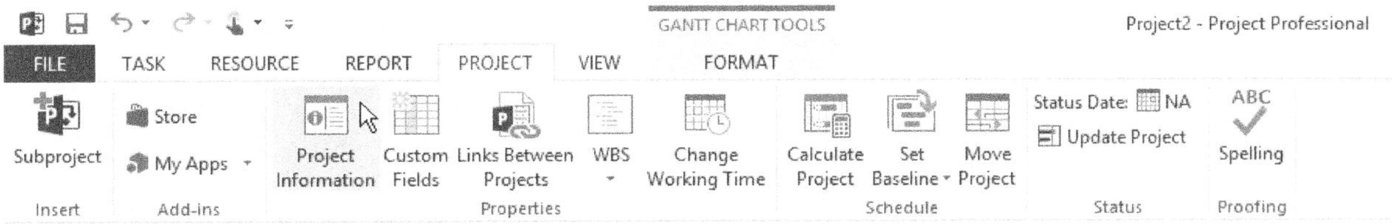


Project opens the *Project Information* dialog box.

Step 2: Select the **Statistics** button.

Project displays the *Project Statistics* dialog box.

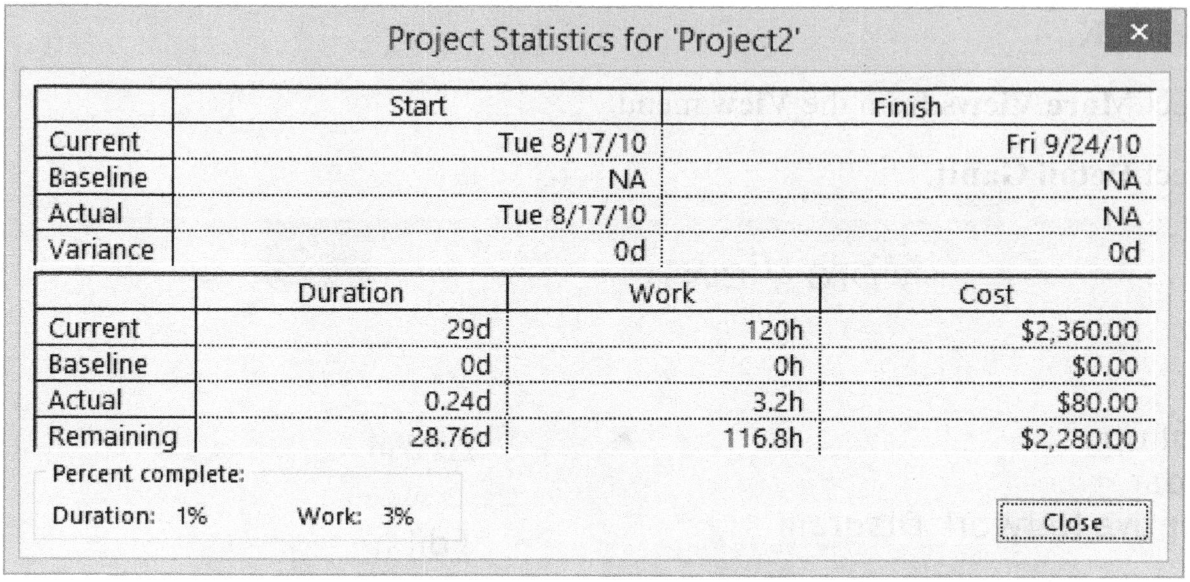
Project Statistics for 'Project2'

| | Start | Finish |
|---|---|---|
| Current | Tue 8/17/10 | Fri 9/24/10 |
| Baseline | NA | NA |
| Actual | Tue 8/17/10 | NA |
| Variance | 0d | 0d |

| | Duration | Work | Cost |
|---|---|---|---|
| Current | 29d | 120h | $2,360.00 |
| Baseline | 0d | 0h | $0.00 |
| Actual | 0.24d | 3.2h | $80.00 |
| Remaining | 28.76d | 116.8h | $2,280.00 |

Percent complete:

Duration: 1% Work: 3%

Close

## Creating a Resource Pool

Step 1: The project that includes the resources becomes the resource pool. Open that file, plus the file that will share resources, which is the sharer project.

Step 2: Select the sharer project from the **Window** area of the **View** tab.

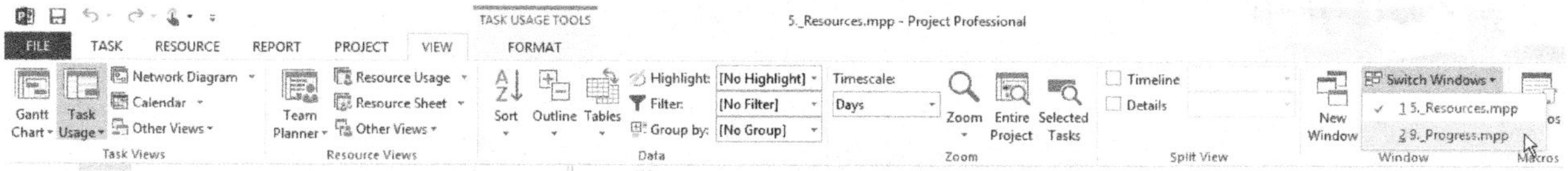


Step 3: Select the **Resource** tab.

Step 4: Select **Resource Pool**.

Step 5: Select **Share Resources**.

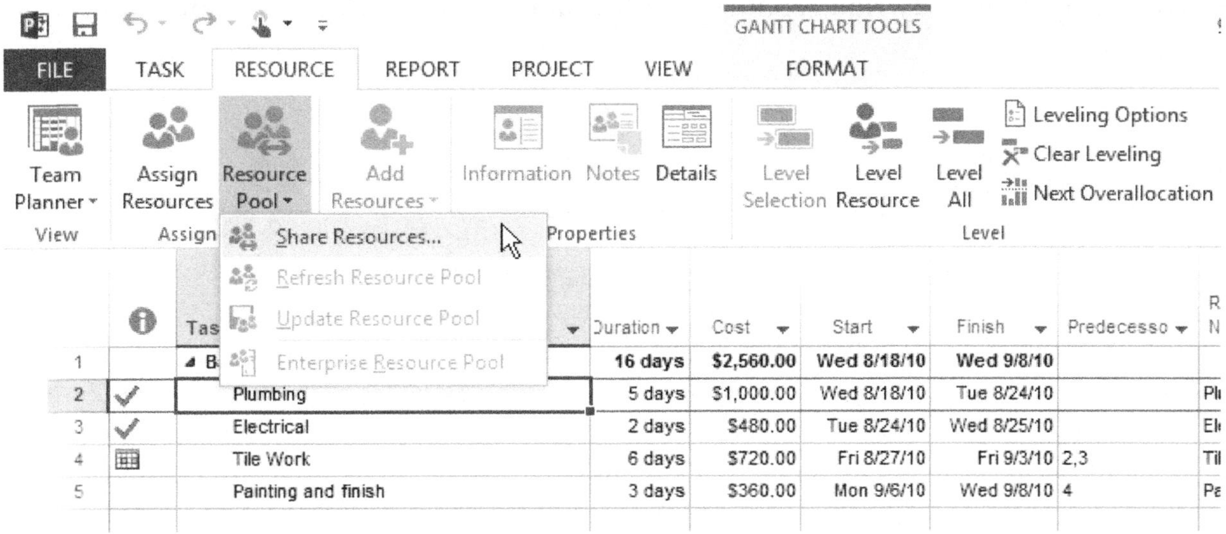


Project displays the Share Resources dialog box.

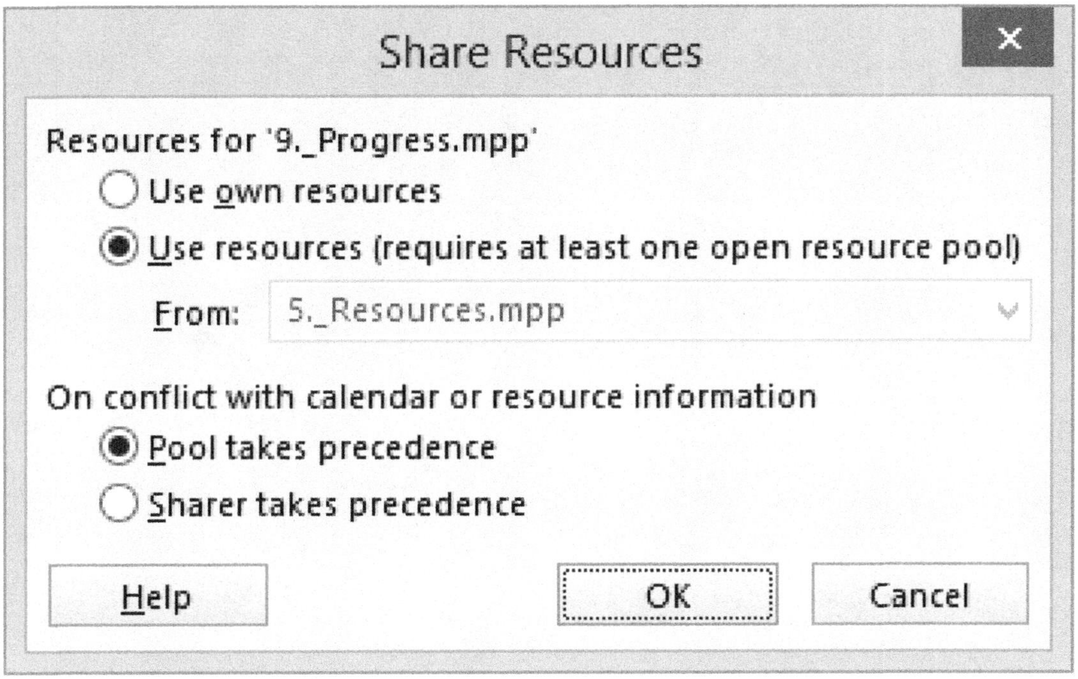


Step 6: Indicate whether to use the project's own resources or the resources from another project. If you select **Use Resources From**, select the project from the drop down list.

Step 7: Select how to handle resource conflicts. This indicates whether to overwrite any duplicate resource information, such as rates.

Step 8: Select **OK**.

View the Resource Sheet to see that the resources are now available to use in the active project. If your project already had resources entered, the resources from both of the projects are combined.

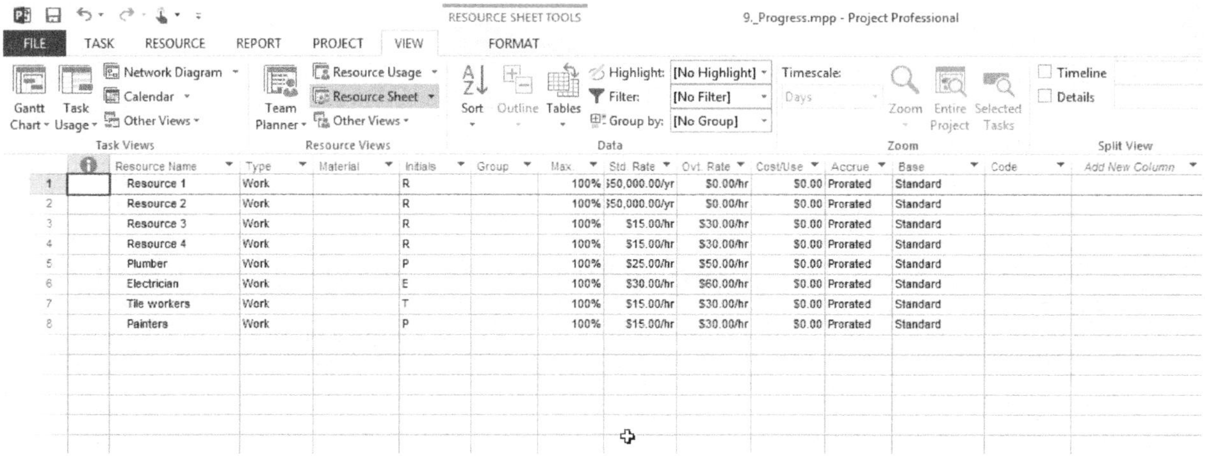

## Additional Titles

The Technical Skill Builder series of books covers a variety of technical application skills. For the availability of titles please see www.silvercitypublications.com/shop/. Note the Master Class volume contains the Essentials, Advanced, and Expert (when available) editions.

## Current Titles

Microsoft Excel 2013 Essentials

Microsoft Excel 2013 Advanced

Microsoft Excel 2013 Expert

Microsoft Excel 2013 Master Class

Microsoft Word 2013 Essentials

Microsoft Word 2013 Advanced

Microsoft Word 2013 Expert

Microsoft Word 2013 Master Class

Microsoft Project 2010 Essentials

Microsoft Project 2010 Advanced

Microsoft Project 2010 Expert

Microsoft Project 2010 Master Class

Microsoft Visio 2010 Essentials

Microsoft Visio 2010 Advanced

Microsoft Visio 2010 Master Class

## Coming Soon

Microsoft Access 2013 Essentials

Microsoft Access 2013 Advanced

Microsoft Access 2013 Expert

Microsoft Access 2013 Master Class

Microsoft PowerPoint 2013 Essentials

Microsoft PowerPoint 2013 Advanced

Microsoft PowerPoint 2013 Expert

Microsoft PowerPoint 2013 Master Class

Microsoft Outlook 2013 Essentials

Microsoft Outlook 2013 Advanced

Microsoft Outlook 2013 Expert

Microsoft Outlook 2013 Master Class

Microsoft Publisher 2010 Essentials

Microsoft Publisher 2010 Advanced

Microsoft Publisher 2010 Master Class

Windows 7 Essentials

Windows 8 Essentials

Made in the USA
Monee, IL
05 November 2026

67383839R00057